General Preface to the Series

Because it is no longer possible for one textbook to cover the whole field of biology while remaining sufficiently up to date, the Institute of Biology proposed this series so that teachers and students can learn about significant developments. The enthusiastic acceptance of 'Studies in Biology' shows that the books are providing authoritative views of biological topics.

The features of the series include the attention given to methods, the selected list of books for further reading and, wherever possible, suggestions for practical work.

Readers' comments will be welcomed by the Education Officer of the Institute.

1984

Institute of Biology
20 Queensberry Place
London SW7 2DZ

Preface to the Second Edition

Animal breeding is not a new activity. From the time of man's early attempts at domestication of reindeer, pigs, goats and other farm species in the Neolithic period (around 7000 B.C.) he has been controlling the mating and reproductive opportunities of these and other species. Throughout man has attempted to change the behaviour, anatomy and morphology of domesticated animals to suit his own requirements. Generally his objectives have not been very precise but the diversity of form, productivity and breadth of productive environment of his domesticated livestock testify to man's success.

During the past seventy years theoretical and experimental studies by Fisher, Haldane, Lush, Wright, their students and others, have established quantitative genetics and animal breeding as recognized branches of biology. The principles on which animal selection should be planned and executed and the expected consequences of such action are now available.

This book sets out some of the principles, gives some results of selection and mating programmes in farm animals and is intended to stimulate an interest in further study of the outstanding problems of animal breeding.

Swindon, 1984

J.C.B.

Contents

The Institute of Biology's
Studies in Biology no. 46

An Introduction to Animal Breeding

Second Edition

John C. Bowman

B.Sc., Ph.D., F.I.Biol.
Secretary, Natural Environment
Research Council

Edward Arnold

© John C. Bowman 1984

First published in Great Britain 1974
by Edward Arnold (Publishers) Ltd
41 Bedford Square, London WC1B 3DQ

Reprinted 1976
Reprinted 1979
Second edition 1984

Edward Arnold (Australia) Pty Ltd
80 Waverley Road
Caulfield East 3145
PO Box 234
Melbourne

First Published in United States of America 1984
By Edward Arnold
300 North Charles Street
Baltimore
Maryland 21201

British Library Cataloguing in Publication Data

Bowman, John C.
    An introduction to animal breeding. – 2nd ed. – (The Institute of Biology's studies in biology; no. 46)
    1. Breeding
    I. Title   II. Series
    636.08'121   SF105

    ISBN 0 7131 2880 1

Typeset by The Castlefield Press, Moulton, Northampton.
Printed and bound in Great Britain at
The Camelot Press Ltd, Southampton

1 Biological Variation

1.1 Introduction

During the past sixty years the productivity of farm livestock has been increasing steadily. To take just two examples, the average number of eggs laid per year by a hen in the U.K. in 1920 was approximately 180; by 1980 the number was 280. Similarly, the average milk production per cow in a single lactation of 305 days was approximately 2500 kg in 1920 and by 1980 was 4500 kg. These changes, and many others of a similar nature and magnitude, have resulted from the combined improved skills of stockmen, animal feed manufacturers, building designers, veterinarians, animal breeders and others. It is difficult to assess quantitatively the contribution each has made to the increased productivity, though as will be seen later it is possible to estimate the genetic change in productivity which the animal breeder has achieved. The aim of the animal breeder, generally, is to change permanently, by selection of suitable individuals in several generations, the mean observed performance (the mean phenotype) of a population. Sometimes the aim may be to reduce, or less often, to increase the variation of phenotype with or without changing the mean phenotype. The phenotype of an animal, is the result of the interacting development of its genotype in its specific environment throughout life from the time of fertilization. Phenotypic differences between individuals may therefore arise from genotypic or environmental differences, or most probably from a combination of both.

Changes between generations in the mean and variation of performance of a population will be permanent, and transmitted to subsequent generations when selection ceases irrespective of changes in the environment, only if the changes have resulted from changes in the mean and variation of the genotypic of the individuals comprising the population.

Selection is the choice of some animals from a larger number of animals on the basis of the differences they show for one or more criteria. The breeder selects between available animals of one generation to decide which shall be allowed to act as parents of the next generation. For selection to be possible there must be phenotypic differences between individuals of the first and each subsequent generation and if selection is to result in permanent changes in phenotypic mean and variation the differences in the base population must be at least partly genotypic.

Therefore primarily the animal breeder is concerned to estimate the nature and magnitude of differences, phenotypic, genotypic and environmental, between individuals in populations. Thereafter any changes in performance which the breeder is able to achieve are limited by the genotypic proportion of these differences.

Examination of most animal species will reveal the existence of phenotypic differences between individuals. For instance, in cattle there are the obvious differences in coat colour and some animals have horns whilst others are hornless or polled. If cattle are weighed or if milk production is recorded there will be differences in performance between individuals. The differences may be classified into two or more categories, depending upon the character examined and upon the units of measurement used. A repeatable and therefore objective or quantifiable measurement of phenotype is a basic necessity for animal or plant breeding. Suppose a population of animals is classified for a single aspect of phenotype, then the proportion of individuals in the several categories can be represented in the form of a frequency histogram as in Fig. 1–1. Those characters for which there are two or only relatively few categories are described as showing discrete variation. For other characters the number of categories is large and limited by the units and accuracy of measurement used for classification. These characters are described as showing continuous variation. The division between characters showing discrete and continuous variation is purely arbitrary. Two category discrete, and continuous variation, are the extremes of a scale of variation which can be found by investigating a number of characters.

For the purpose of genetic interpretation of the biological variation, those characters which are classed as showing discrete variation are considered to be controlled by few genes. It was on characters showing discrete variation that Mendel developed his theories of genetic control and segregation. When later workers attempted to apply Mendelian principles to characters showing continuous variation, they encountered severe problems of interpretation. Early attempts were made to subdivide characters such as milk production and egg production into sub-characters, which might be amenable to genetic interpretation in Mendelian terms. Such efforts were largely unsuccessful.

It is now considered that characters showing continuous variation are controlled by many loci, the genes of which act according to Mendelian principles. Extrapolation from phenotype back to chromosomal gene is often inappropriate even for characters showing discrete variation, since the physiological processes involved between the two stages are extremely complex. Similarly, extrapolation for characters showing continuous variation is even more inappropriate. However, a body of mathematical theory was developed, by Wright, Fisher, Lush and others, to interpret the genetic control of characters showing continuous variation. This approach has been shown by experiment to be substantially satisfactory in describing biological variation under different environmental circumstances and in predicting changes in means and variations of populations under selection. The theory assumes that the genes at any one locus act according to Mendelian principles and that the genetic control of a quantitative character is the result of the combined action of many loci. As will be seen later, the forms of combined action included in the theory are few and simple. In view of the rapidly increasing knowledge of chromosome and gene biochemistry and of the physiological processes which

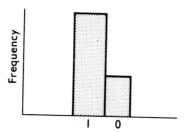

Scale of measurement

e.g. in cattle; horned· = I, polled = 0

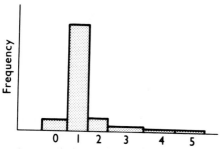

Scale of measurement

e.g. in cattle; the number of live calves per calving

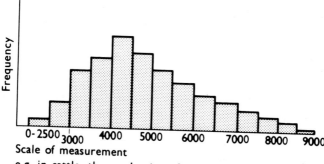

Scale of measurement

e.g. in cattle, the production of milk per lactation in kg

Fig. 1–1 Frequency histograms.

occur during the development of an animal it may be that more sophisticated forms of combined gene action will have to be included in the theory. However, operationally the mathematical approach has proved successful in both animal and plant breeding. It is essential to see this approach as an operational tool and being representative of genetic knowledge at the present time and not as an explanation of observed biological variation.

2 Mendelian Genetics and Gene Frequencies

Although the animal breeder is principally concerned with characters showing continuous variation, he also has to deal with characters controlled by relatively few genes, each having a comparatively large effect. A few examples will serve to illustrate some of the simpler but important principles of Mendelian genetics and the way these principles can be applied when the animal breeder wishes to change gene frequencies by selection.

2.1 Additive gene action

The first example concerns the breed of poultry known as the Blue Andalusian fowl. The plumage of birds of this breed can be classified quite easily into three categories. There are those birds which have totally white plumage, those birds which have totally black plumage and a third group which is known as the true Blue Andalusian fowl. The genetics of this feather pattern are simple. The totally white and totally black groups are the homozygotes and the Blue Andalusian fowl is the heterozygote. It so happens that without knowing it the breed society concerned with Blue Audalusian fowl selected the heterozygote as the standard for the breed. All birds which show completely white or completely black feathering are discarded and only those birds showing the mingled feather pattern are used as parents of the following generation. The result is that the progeny of intermatings of Blue Andalusian fowl come out in the ratio of 1:2:1 for white, blue and black feathering respectively. It is obviously quite impossible to fix the breed type and 50% of the population must be selected against in each generation. However, the example serves to illustrate the point that the black and white genes responsible for the two homozygous categories of feather pattern act additively when combined in the heterozygote. This is one of the rare cases where the heterozygote is apparent and can easily be observed to be intermediated between the two homozygous categories.

2.2 Recessive-dominance gene action

A more frequently observed situation is that in which one allele is recessive to the alternative allele. One example from poultry and another from cattle will show how the animal breeder can make use of this principle and also some of the difficulties involved in fixing the dominant allele in the homozygous state. Amongst breeds of poultry used for meat production there are a pair of alleles which give either yellow-skinned birds or white-skinned birds. The gene for white skin is dominant to that for yellow skin. During the past 30 years much effort has been put into selecting meat strains of poultry for improved growth rate and feed conversion. Most of this development work was carried out in the United States, and though selection programmes were carried out in the United Kingdom they were started relatively late. When in 1962 importation of strains of poultry was allowed into the United Kingdom for the first time many of the better American poultry strains were imported into the U.K. The American housewife preferred yellow-skinned broilers whereas the British housewife showed a marked preference for white-skinned ones. Most of the American poultry strains imported into the U.K., though extremely good on growth rate and feed conversion efficiency, were yellow skinned, whereas the strains selected in the U.K. were white skinned. It was therefore necessary to transfer the white skin gene from the British poultry strains to the American poultry strains without, at the same time, losing the advantage in terms of growth rate and feed conversion of the American populations.

The gene transfer was accomplished in the following way. A first cross was made between white-skinned British strains and yellow-skinned American strains. All the F_1 progeny were white skinned but heterozygous. F_1 intercross matings were made and the F_2 progeny were white and yellow skinned in the ratio of 3:1. The F_2 yellow-skinned progeny were discarded. The problem which then arose was to decide which of the white-skinned progeny were homozygous and which were heterozygous for the white gene. Though the distinction could obviously not be made phenotypically it was possible to make the genotypic distinction by means of a simple progeny test. White-skinned males of unknown genotype were mated to yellow-skinned females which were obviously homozygous for the yellow gene. Those individuals which were homozygous for the white gene would have only white-skinned progeny whereas those which were heterozygous for the white-skinned gene would have both yellow- and white-skinned progeny. On the basis of the progeny skin colour it was then easy to isolate the homozygous white-skinned parents and to establish a pure breeding white-skinned population which also carried many of the genes for growth rate and feed conversion which had come from the American strains.

The second example of the value of a dominant-recessive pair of alleles comes from cattle. The Hereford breed of cattle has a white face pattern which is controlled by a single dominant gene. Hereford cattle are largely maintained for the production of bulls for crossing with other breeds of cattle, particularly dairy cattle, to produce crossbred calves for veal and beef production. The crossbred calves produced from Hereford bulls all have the white face pattern which distinguishes the breed. In this way it is easy to distinguish Hereford crossbred progeny which can be used for beef production and cannot therefore be used for breeding replacements for the dairy herd for which they would be entirely unsuitable. This is a good example of a colour marking gene being used to distinguish progeny of different types. It may be considered as a very useful hereditary trade mark. A similar gene is present in Simmental cattle.

2.3 Overdominance

This term refers to a situation at a locus in which the phenotypic expression of the heterozygote exceeds that of either of the homozygotes. A good example of this situation is to be found in the White Wyandotte breed of poultry. The breed contains two types of head comb, namely rose and single, which are determined by a single pair of genes. The gene for rose comb, R, is dominant to the gene for single comb, r. The phenotype set as a standard for the breed was rose comb and for many years it was not understood why the single comb persisted in the breed when it was selected against. New mutation would not account for the frequency of the single comb phenotype in the population.

It has now been shown that the fertility of homozygous rose (RR) comb males is lower than that of the other two genotypes and in particular than heterozygous rose (Rr) comb males. The lowered fertility of the RR males is not an effect of the rose gene in the sperm cell but is caused by the RR male host body affecting the fertility and the duration of fertilizing ability of the sperm cells. Thus the effect of this locus on the phenotype of the breed may be summarized as:

	Genotype and comb phenotype		
	RR, rose	Rr, rose	rr, single
Males	Lower fertility	Normal fertility	Normal fertility
Females	Normal fertility	Normal fertility	Normal fertility

Taking into account the breed standard, those males having the desired combination of correct comb type and normal fertility are the heterozygous rose comb individuals. Both homozygous and heterozygous rose comb females are satisfactory. Thus the effect of selection would be that most of the progeny of the breed would be produced from heterozygous rose comb males which would maintain the single comb gene in the population and which in matings with heterozygous rose comb females would produce a quarter of their progeny with single combs. Under the conditions created by the breed standard the heterozygous males show overdominance.

2.4 Epistasis

This term refers to the situation in which there is interaction between the genes at two or more loci, so that the phenotype for a particular trait is determined by more than one locus, collectively acting non-additively. A well-documented example of this is the genetic control of comb types in poultry. We have already seen that there are single and rose combs, but there are also pea and walnut combs. The pea comb is determined by a gene dominant to a gene for single comb at a separate locus to the rose gene locus. A walnut comb results in any individual in which at least one rose and one pea gene are present. Thus the genotypes and phenotypes can be designated as follows:

		Rose comb locus		
		RR	Rr	rr
	PP	RRPP	RrPP	rrPP
Pea		walnut	walnut	pea
Comb	Pp	RRPp	RrPp	rrPp
Locus		walnut	walnut	pea
	pp	RRpp	Rrpp	rrpp
		rose	rose	single

This is a simple example of two loci interaction. In practice we assume that such interactions between many loci do occur in determining the overall phenotype of an animal.

2.5 Sex linkage

The principle of sex linkage has also been put to commercial use in the poultry industry. The genetics of the silver, gold pair of alleles responsible for the production of the feather colours indicated by their name, was worked out by Pease and Punnet in the 1920s. The silver gene which occurs in the Light Sussex breed of poultry is dominant to gold, which occurs in the Rhode Island Red and New Hampshire breeds. The genes are on the sex chromosomes and in poultry the female is the heterogametic sex. If homozygous gold cockerels of the Rhode Island Red or New Hampshire breed are mated to silver females of the Light Sussex breed the progeny have the following feather colour. All the male progeny will be heterozygous and will be silver whereas the female progeny will carry a single allele and will be gold. In this instance, the colour of the feathers is also reflected in the colour of the down of the day-old chick. Those chicks which are male are white whereas those which are female have a brownish tinge to the down. It is, therefore, possible by observation of the colour of the down to distinguish at birth the sex of progeny of matings of this type. In the poultry industry in the course of the production of day-old chicks destined for laying production, it is advisable to identify the sexes at birth. The males can then be destroyed without incurring further cost and the females can be reared on their own. Similarly in the broiler industry there are advantages to be gained in terms of growth rate and carcase quality by rearing sexes separately. If it is not possible to use a sex linked gene pair to distinguish the sexes at birth, it is necessary to employ sexers in the hatchery to carry out this job by means of vent sexing. This has the disadvantage that it is expensive, time-consuming in the hatchery and may cause some damage to the day-old chick.

2.6 Multiple allelism

All the genetic situations discussed above have been concerned with loci involving only two alleles. As in man, the blood groups of domesticated farm animals have been investigated. In all species it appears that the blood groups are controlled by alleles at relatively few loci (perhaps of the order of 8 to 20). However, it is clear that at each locus there are a considerable number of possible alleles. For instance, at the B locus in cattle well over 200 alleles are known. Similarly in poultry at the B blood group locus over 20 alleles are known. In most cases it is possible to distinguish heterozygotes. A considerable amount of research has been carried out to find out why multiple allelism should be so widespread for these genes. No satisfactory answers have yet been produced, but it is clear that blood group alleles are implicated in pre- and post-natal survival and probably with disease resistance. Though many questions with regard to the blood groups still need to be answered, the knowledge gained so far has enabled the animal breeder to put the blood groups to good use. Even with the few loci involved the existence of multiple allelism means that a very large number of genotypes are possible. By means of regular blood typing of individuals and strains of farm animals the breeder is able to check the pedigree of the animals in a breeding programme. In cattle where artificial insemination is in widespread use, it is extremely easy for the inseminator to make a mistake and use the wrong semen on a cow. By typing of the bull, cow and progeny, it is possible to determine whether the calf could be the progeny of the matings stated in the records. In the course of checking on mating records in poultry breeding programmes, it has been found that approximately 3% of pedigree records are in error. The knowledge of a comparatively simple multiple allelic situation can thus be turned into an extremely valuable parentage testing scheme.

2.7 Quantification of selection at a single locus

The examples quoted above have illustrated how the animal breeder has made commercial application of simple Mendelian knowledge. The same principles apply to the inheritance of characters showing continuous variation. It is appropriate, therefore, before proceeding to a study of continuous variation, to quantify in algebraic terms the examples which have just been discussed. Consider a single locus situation at which there are two alleles. The two alleles are J and j and the gene frequencies are p and q respectively, such that $p + q = 1$ for a population. According to the Hardy-Weinberg equilibrium and for a population in the idealized state the genotypic frequencies would be as follows:

Genotype	JJ	Jj	jj
Frequencies	p^2	$2pq$	q^2

The conditions which specify an idealized population may be stated as:

(i)   Mating is restricted to individuals within a single population. It is not possible for individuals to mate with individuals of a second population. In brief, migration of individuals is excluded.

(ii) The generations do not overlap so that it is not possible for individuals of one generation to mate with individuals of either the previous or following generations.

(iii) The population size remains the same from one generation to the next.

(iv) Mating within the population is completely at random and in the discussion which follows includes self-fertilization. This is obviously not possible in the case of animals and allowance is sometimes made for this fact.

(v)   There is no selection. The number of progeny produced is equal to the number of parents used in the previous generation.

(vi) Mutation, though it is known to occur, is assumed to be absent so far as the idealized population is concerned.

It is realized that the conditions of the idealized population rarely if ever occur in practice, though it is generally assumed that the Hardy-Weinburg equilibrium is widely applicable to breeding populations. Suppose that selection is applied to a population in Hardy-Weinburg equilibrium, and that the locus concerned shows additivity. Selection implies that an individual selected against has a reduced opportunity of leaving progeny in the following generation. In the extreme situation the individuals selected against are killed and leave no progeny. The ability to leave progeny can be looked at in terms of fitness. The individual which is selected has a fitness of 1, whereas the individual selected against has a comparative fitness of $(1-S)$ where S represents the degree of selection, with a value between 0 and 1. When all individuals of the unwanted phenotype are discarded $S = 1$. Suppose there is a situation in which selection is in favour of the J and against the j gene. The relative fitness of the three possible genotypes can be written as follows:

Genotype	JJ	Jj	jj
Relative fitness	1	$1-\frac{1}{2}S$	$1-S$

By means of the relative fitness values and the gene frequencies for the three genotypes the genotypic frequencies in the next generation can be calculated. The difference between the gene frequencies in the two generations represents the change of gene frequency, Δq, from one generation to the next.

Frequency of $J = p$ and of $j = q$ such that $p + q = 1$

Generation 1	JJ	Jj	jj
Genotypic frequency	p^2	$2pq$	q^2
Relative fitness	1	$1-\frac{1}{2}S$	$1-S$
Gametic contributions after selection	p^2	$2pq(1-\frac{1}{2}S)$	$q^2(1-S)$

It will be noted that the genotypic frequencies are in proportionate terms and in the first generation are equal to unity. After selection the gametic contribution is no longer unity but equals

$$1 - pqS - q^2S = 1 - Sq\,(p + q) = 1 - Sq$$

In order to calculate the gene frequency of j in the next generation, the sum of the gametic contributions of the appropriate genotypes must be taken as a proportion of the new total gametic contribution. Thus the frequency of j in generation 2 is

$$\frac{\frac{1}{2}[2pq\,(1 - \frac{1}{2}S)] + q^2\,(1 - S)}{1 - Sq} = \frac{q - \frac{1}{2}Sq^2 - \frac{1}{2}Sq}{1 - Sq}$$

Therefore the change in frequency of the j allele from one generation to the next

$$\Delta q = \frac{q - \frac{1}{2}Sq^2 - \frac{1}{2}Sq}{1 - Sq} - q = \frac{-\frac{1}{2}Sq\,(1 - q)}{1 - Sq}$$

Other formulae can be derived similarly for loci at which there is some specified level of dominance and for selection against specified genotypes.

For instance with selection for and complete dominance of J, the relative fitnesses of JJ, Jj and jj are 1, 1 and $1-S$ respectively and the change in gene frequency of the j allele from one generation to the next

$$\Delta q = \frac{-Sq^2\,(1 - q)}{1 - Sq^2}$$

Notice that artifical selection is usually applied to complete genotypes but the effect is to change both genotype and gene frequencies.

With the aid of these formulae, and knowing the starting gene frequencies and selection pressure applied, it is possible to estimate the rate of change of gene frequency and how many generations it will take to produce a homozygous population. In the case of selection in favour of heterozygotes, homozygosity may never be obtained and depending on the selection pressures an intermediate equilibrium gene frequency may be reached and stabilized.

3 Quantitative Genetics and Heritability

3.1 The binomial and normal distributions

An understanding of some elementary probability theory and statistics is necessary for an appreciation of the mathematical approach to selection. The binomial distribution is the frequency distribution obtained by use of the binomial expansion. If a is the probability of a positive event in a single trial and b is the probability of a negative or opposite event in a single trial, then the respective probabilities of $0, 1, 2 \ldots w$ positive events in a specified number of trials involving w events is given by the successive terms of the binomial expansion of $(a + b)^w$. These terms are: $(a + b)$, $(a^2 + 2ab + b^2)$, $(a^3 + 3a^2b + 3ab^2 + b^3)$, $(a^4 + 4a^3b + 6a^2b^2 + 4ab^3 + b^4)$, etc. For example, suppose that the probability that the sex of a piglet at birth is male is 0.5 and therefore the probability that it is female is also 0.5. Thus a and $b = 0.5$. Suppose that it is desired to calculate the probability of different combinations of sexes for litters of different sizes in pigs. The appropriate probabilities of the number of males and females in litters of 8 piglets are given in Fig. 3–1. Thus for a litter size of 8, on average only 1 litter in 128 will be composed of either all males or all females. Similarly, for the same litter size, on average 70 litters out of 256 will be composed of 4 males and 4 females. Direct observation of litters of pigs and scoring of the sex ratio may give a distribution slightly different from that expected from Fig. 3–1. There are at least two reasons for the discrepancy. Firstly the probabilities in Fig. 3–1 are the average probabilities expected on the basis of several hundred observations, and it is unlikely that in any set of data there will be sufficient observations to obtain an exact correspondence with the expected situation. This is often referred to as the sampling effect. Secondly the probability that a piglet at birth will be male or female is not exactly equal and in practice a would equal 0.526 and b would therefore equal 0.474. Then $a^2 \neq ab \neq b^2$, etc., and the terms of the expansion would not be symmetrical as in the example quoted.

To return to the symmetrical case, where $a = b = 0.5$, we may represent the expansion terms in the form of a frequency histogram as in Fig. 3–1 where the example of a litter size of 8 pigs is shown. As w gets larger and larger the shape of the tops of the columns of the histogram approach a bell-shaped curve. This limiting frequency is known as the normal frequency curve. If the frequencies are converted into relative frequencies or probabilities, the normal frequency curve becomes a normal probability curve. This curve can be used to represent the continuous variation shown by many characters of importance to the animal breeder. Such characters are described as having variation distributed about the mean according to the normal distribution.

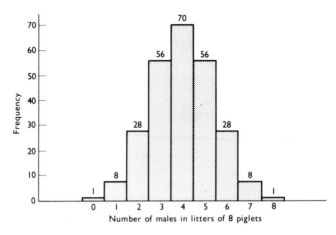

Fig. 3–1 Frequency histograms for binominal expansions of $w = a = b = 0.5$.

In a theoretical situation in which all differences in a quantitative character between individuals in a population are genetic, the normal distribution can be considered to represent the distribution of relative frequencies of individuals carrying different numbers of positive and negative alleles for the character. Thus if, in the binomial expansion, a represents the mean frequency of positive alleles and b represents the mean frequency of negative alleles, at the w loci affecting the character, then the terms of the expansion represent the relative frequencies of individuals having values ranging from a^w to b^w. It has been assumed that positive (or negative) genes at different loci have equal effect and that there is no dominance or non-allelic interaction. In the biological situation the actual distribution will result from combinations of additive gene action, dominance, epistasis and extraneous variation caused by many environmental factors. Hence the normal distribution is used to represent the distribution of phenotypic values of a character. A few standard parameters are used to describe the normal distribution. These are the mean, the variance and the standard deviation (see HEATH, 1970).

3.2 Partitioning the phenotypic variance

The variance calculated from a set of observed values is known as the phenotypic variance, σ_P^2. It is the sum of the variances attributable to genetic and environmental sources and the interaction between them. This may be represented as:

$$\sigma_P^2 = \sigma_G^2 + \sigma_E^2 + \sigma_{GE}^2 + \sigma_W^2$$

where σ_G^2 = variance of genetic differences between individuals.
σ_E^2 = variance of specified environmental differences between individuals.

σ_{GE}^2 = variance of the interaction of genotype and specified environment.
σ_W^2 = variance of the unspecified environmental differences between individuals.

In other words, individuals have different phenotypes because their genotypes are different and because they are exposed during development from the time of fertilization to different environments. Some of the differences in environment to which individuals are exposed can be specified (e.g. different nutritional regimes, disease control measures, soil types, climates, housing systems) whilst others cannot be specified and these include errors of observation and measurement of the character concerned. It is possible by means of suitable statistical methods to obtain quantitative estimates of these several sources of variance. Estimates can also be obtained from data on mono- and di-zygous twins in cattle and man but the estimates are subject to certain biases which render them less useful than those obtained from other types of genetically related individuals. The biases are associated with the fact that such twins tend to seek more similar environments than would groups of less closely related individuals, and because they share a common pre-natal environment.

However, twins have been used to demonstrate the relative magnitude of genetic and enviromental herd differences for several production traits in dairy cattle. The experiment to be described was partly conducted at and organized from the Ruakara Animal Research Station in New Zealand, and its objective was to determine the extent of the genetic differences existing among a sample of the dairy herds of New Zealand. The experiment was organized in two parts. In one part, 240 young calves were taken from 40 herds, half of which had high average milk production and half of which had low average milk production. The calves were taken to Ruakara and reared and milked as a uniformly treated herd of cattle. In the second part, 120 sets of monozygous twin calves were divided amongst the 40 herds so that one member of a twin pair went to a high producing herd and the other member went to a low producing herd, to replace the calves taken to Ruakara. Full performance records were collected on all calves in the experiment and on all animals in the 40 herds. Assumptions underlying the records were as follows. Any difference between the calves from high and low producing herds kept on a common environment at Ruakara would be caused by genetic differences between the two types of herd. Any differences between the twins of a pair, which are genetically identical, reared and producing in high and low herds, would represent environmental differences between the herds. Some of the results are given in Table 1. The slightly different representation of sample herds in the Ruakara and twin results is the cause of the different herd averages in the two cases. The records from the calves reared at Ruakara show that all of the herd differences for milk production and for days in milk are environmental whereas 44% and 10% of the differences in fat test and fat yield respectively are genetic. The records from the twin calves indicate that 97% and 89% of the differences in milk yield and days in milk respectively are

Table 1 Results of a Ruakura twin experiment.

Part 1 Comparison of herds and their calves transferred to Ruakura.

	Herd performance*			Calves at Ruakura from			Ruakura difference / Herd difference / i.e. genetic difference
	high	low	diff.	high	low	diff.	
Milk yield (kg)	2813	1960	853	2728	2736	−8	−0.01
Fat test (%)	5.51	5.12	0.39	5.50	5.33	0.17	0.44
Fat yield (kg)	154.9	100.1	54.8	149.8	144.5	5.3	0.10
Days in milk	284.5	249.3	35.2	296.0	297.4	−1.4	−0.04

Part II Comparison of herds and split twin pairs transferred to herds.

	Herd Performance*			Twins in herds			Twin difference / Herd difference / i.e. environmental difference
	high	low	diff.	high	low	diff.	
Milk yield (kg)	2788	1984	804	2639	1856	783	0.97
Fat test (%)	5.50	5.10	0.40	5.26	5.11	0.15	0.38
Fat yield (kg)	153.4	101.1	52.3	139.0	94.7	44.3	0.85
Days in milk	285.5	249.8	35.7	278.8	247.0	31.8	0.89

*The slightly different representation of parent herds in the Ruakura and twin results is the cause of the different averages in the two cases. (Adapted from Table 5 of BRUMBY, 1961, *Animal Production*, **3**, 277–94; by kind permission of the author and the editor.)

environmental whereas the percentage drops to 38% and 85% for fat test and fat yield. The results from the two parts of the experiment are in good accord except for the figures on fat test. Other records from the experiment indicated no genetic differences for body size and fertility between cattle in the high- and low-producing herds.

Estimates of the proportion of the phenotypic differences which are genetic are important to the animal breeder. Only if there are genetic differences is it possible to undertake worthwhile selection programmes. The results of the Ruakara experiment mean that the breeder would not obtain cattle with higher milk production by selecting animals from herds with high as compared to low average milk production. It is just as likely that genetically superior cattle for milk production would be obtained by selecting the highest producing animals from low as well as high average herds. Selection would need to be on a within herd basis in order to avoid the environmental differences between herds. If, alternatively, the breeder's objective was improved fat yield instead of milk yield then there would be some advantage in selecting the animals with the highest fat yield from those herds with the highest average fat yield because some portion of the herd differences are genetic. Thus it is important to have some knowledge of the source and distribution of variance before commencing any selection. A simple division into genetic and environmental variance as indicated by the Ruakara experiment is not usually adequate for the breeder and a more detailed breakdown of the variance of the type to be discussed later is required.

3.3 Regression and correlation

There are many instances in animal production in which variation in environmental factors gives rise to simultaneous variation in the animals' performance. For instance, the milk yield in the first lactation of a cow increases as the age at calving increases. A relationship of this type in which for a unit change in the environmental factor there is some corresponding change in the animal performance is known as a correlation. The factor which causes the correlation is known as the independent variate whereas the factor which is affected is known as the dependent variate. When an increase or decrease in the independent variate results in a corresponding increase or decrease in the dependent variate, the correlation is positive. However, in those cases where an increase or decrease in the independent variate leads to corresponding decreases or increases in the dependent variate then the correlation is negative. Two parameters quantify the relationship between the independent and the dependent variates. These two parameters are known as the linear regression coefficient and the correlation coefficient. The regression coefficient is the best estimate of the multiplicand needed to predict the value of one variate from the value of a related variate. Its value can be positive or negative and is unlimited. The correlation coefficient is an estimate of the extent to which two variates vary together and it can have a value ranging from +1 through zero to −1. The square of the correlation coefficient is an estimate of the proportion of the variation which is common to the two variates. For instance, a correlation coefficient of 0.6 would mean that 36% of the variation of the dependent variate could be accounted for by variation of the independent variate.

Regression and correlation are used to quantify several different situations of importance to the animal breeder. For instance, the example already quoted refers to the effect of changes in environment on a phenotypic character. A relationship of frequent importance is that between two phenotypic characters in the same individuals. Suppose on a group of cattle that both the weight of the animals and their milk yield are recorded. Then it is possible to calculate the regression of milk yield on body weight and the correlation between the two characters. The correlation calculated from the phenotypic values is referred to as the phenotypic correlation. Now the relationship between the two characters may be caused largely for two separate reasons, one environmental and one genetic. If those factors in the environment which affect milk yield also affect body weight, then some of the variance of the two characters will be common. Similarly if some genes have effects on both characters (there is pleiotropy) or if genes affecting the two characters are linked on the same chromosomes then again there will be some variation common to both characters. Thus the phenotypic correlation (r_P) is dependent on an environmental correlation (r_E) and a genetic correlation (r_G). The relationship between the three is not simple and they may differ in sign as well as in value for the same pair of characters.

A genetic correlation caused by pleiotrophy is permanent and cannot be altered by selection whereas one caused by linkage is transient and may change in time as a consequence of selection and crossing over during meiosis. The main value of genetic correlations is to predict the changes in character not being directly selected but correlated to the character being directly selected as will be described in Chapter 5.

Another type of genetic correlation is that calculated from paired readings for the same character in related individuals such as in sire and son or dam and offspring. A correlation in this case results from the fact that the related individuals have a known proportion of their genes in common.

3.4 Quantitative gene action

So far we have observed that a population exhibiting continuous variation can be described in terms of the mean and phenotypic variance of the population. The variance has been partitioned into genetic and environmental components. We have noted that it is assumed that quantitative characters are controlled by the action of genes at several loci, that the genes at these loci may act additively or express various degrees of dominance (intralocular interaction) and that there may be various types of interaction between genes at different loci (epistasis or interlocular interaction). Normally it is not possible to estimate the number of genes and loci nor the gene frequencies at the loci affecting a quantitative character. The only observations which can be made usually concern the measurement of the phenotype and the pedigree relationship of individuals in a population and from one generation to the next. Now the problem is to relate in quantitative terms the assumptions concerning the quantitative actions and the frequencies of the genes controlling a character to those parameters of an individual and of the population to which it belongs, which can be estimated from the phenotypic measurements.

Let us consider a single locus, two allele case such that the frequency of alleles J and j is p and q respectively. Let the quantitative values be a and $-a$ for the two homozygotes such that the mean value of the two homozygotes is 0. The value of the homozygote is d which may have any value, depending on the form of gene action at the locus. This situation may be represented as follows:

Genotype	JJ	Jj	jj
Value	a	d	$-a$
Frequency (at equilibrium for an idealized population)	p^2	$2pq$	q^2

For additive gene action $d = 0$, for partial dominance $d>0$ and $<(a$ or $-a)$, for full dominance $D = (a$ or $-a)$ and for overdominance $d>(a$ or $-a)$.

The mean value of the population can be obtained as the product of the frequency and the value of each genotype, and summing over genotypes. As the frequency is already in proportion there is no need to divide the sum by the number of observations.

The mean value $= ap^2 + d2pq + (-a)q^2 = a(p^2 - q^2) + 2dpq = a(p - q) + 2dpq$

If more than one locus is involved and is assumed that there is no epistasis then the total quantitative effect is the sum of the effects of the individual loci which may be expressed as

$$\text{Mean value} = \Sigma a(p - q) + 2\Sigma dpq$$

The variance may be obtained as the product of the frequency and the (value of each genotype, expressed as a deviation from mean)² and summing over genotypes.

Therefore variance $=\ p^2[a - \{a(p - q) + 2dpq\}]^2$
$+ 2pq[d - \{a(p - q) + 2dpq\}]^2$
$+ q^2[-a - \{a(p - q) + 2dpq\}]^2$

which may be expressed as

$$\text{Variance} = 2pq[a + d(q - p)]^2 + [2pqd]^2$$

The summation is over all loci involved, no epistasis is assumed and this is the variance of genotypic values, or σ_G^2. How does the genotypic variance relate to the several forms of intra- and inter-locular gene action? It is necessary to define three terms, namely: (*i*) average gene effect; (*ii*) breeding value; (*iii*) dominance deviation.

The 'average gene effect' as defined by FALCONER (1981) is the mean deviation from the population mean of individuals which received that gene from one parent, the gene received from the other parent having come at random from the population. In other words it is the average quantitative effect of substituting one allele for its alternative, and this is given in terms of genotypic values and frequencies below. The frequency of gene $J = p$ and of $j = q$ and $p + q = 1$.

Type of gamete	Values and frequencies of genotypes produced			Mean values of genotypes produced	Population mean to be deducted	Average effect of gene
	JJ a	Jj d	jj $-a$			
J	p	q		$pa + qd$	$- [a(p - q) + 2dpq]$	$q[a + d(q - p)]$
j		p	q	$-qa + pd$	$- [a(p - q) + 2dpq]$	$-p[a + d(q - p)]$

(From FALCONER, 1981, *Introduction to Quantitative Genetics*. Longman, London.)

Thus the average effect of gene J is, $q[a + d(q - p)]$
and of gene j is, $- p[a + d(q - p)]$.

Summation of the average gene effects over both alleles at each locus and for all the loci which determine the character considered is referred to as the 'breeding value' of the individual. The breeding value represent the quantitative effect of the additive gene action at the loci affecting the character. Thus breeding values of genotypes at a single locus are as follows:

Genotype	Breeding value
JJ	$2q[a + d(q - p)]$
Jj	$(q - p)[a + d(q - p)]$
jj	$-2p[a + d(q - p)]$

These values are still expressed as deviations from population mean so that the mean breeding value of a population is zero.

Finally the dominance deviation is the difference between the breeding value and the genotypic value, each expressed as a deviation from population mean.

For example, the genotypic value of *JJ* is a, and expressed as a deviation from population mean it is $2q(a-dp)$. The breeding value as a deviation from population mean is $2q[a+d(q-p)]$ and therefore the difference between them, which is $-2dq^2$, represents the dominance deviation or quantitative effect of dominance at the loci affecting the character. For all genotypes the values are as follows:

Genotypes	Frequency	Genotypic values	Expressed as a deviation from population mean Genotypic value	Breeding value	Dominance deviation
JJ	p^2	a	$2q(a-pq)$	$2q[a+d(q-p)]$	$-2dq^2$
Jj	$2pq$	d	$a(q-p)+d(1-2pq)$	$(q-p)[a+d(q-p)]$	$2dpq$
jj	q^2	$-a$	$-2p(a+qd)$	$-2p[a+d(q-p)]$	$-2dp^2$

The sum of the breeding values and dominance deviations expressed in this way is zero. As the breeding values and dominance deviations have been expressed as deviations from population mean, it is easy to calculate their variances.

Thus the variance of breeding values (or of additive gene effects) is

$$p^2(2q[a+d(q-p)])^2+2pq((q-p)[a+d(q-p)])^2+q^2(-2p[a+d(q-p)])^2$$

which reduces to

$$2pq[a+d(q-p)]^2$$

This is referred to as the additive genetic variance or σ_A^2. Similarly the variance of dominance deviations is

$$p^2(-2dq^2)^2+2pq(2dpq)^2+q^2(-2dp^2)^2$$

which reduces to

$$(2pqd)^2$$

This is referred to as the dominance variance or σ_D^2. We note that the sum of these two variances is equal to the genotypic variance. Thus

$$\sigma_G^2 = \sigma_A^2 + \sigma_D^2$$

The values of these variances are maximal when gene frequencies are in the range 0.3 to 0.7 and decline to zero as gene frequencies tend to homozygosity.

Consideration of quantitative gene effects so far has been in the terms of a model which assumed additivity between the effects of the several loci affecting the character concerned. The formulae above refer to gene frequency and genotypic values for a single locus, and modifications required to the formulae to make them applicable to the multiloci case merely involved summation of effects across loci. However, as has been indicated in Chapter 2, genes at different loci do not always act additively and various forms of interaction have been studied and shown to exist. Therefore if the model assumes epistasis to be present this is an additional source of variation, which is designated interaction variance or σ_I^2, and the genotypic variance is then $\sigma^2{}_G = \sigma_A^2 + \sigma_D^2 + \sigma_I^2$

Substituting this expression into the composition of the phenotypic variance we find that

$$\sigma_P^2 = \sigma_A^2 + \sigma_D^2 + \sigma_I^2 + \sigma_{GE}^2 + \sigma_E^2 + \sigma_W^2 \text{ (See page 12)}$$

3.5 Heritability

The proportion which the additive genetic variance, σ_A^2, represents of the phenotypic variance, σ_P^2, is referred to as the heritability.

Thus $h^2 = \dfrac{\sigma_A^2}{\sigma_P^2}$ which can have any value from 0 to 1.

It can be shown that the heritability is also equal to the regression coefficient of breeding value on phenotypic value. It is possible by means of several suitable statistical methods applied to data from individuals whose pedigree relationships are known (e.g. information from groups of half brothers or sisters or from daughter-dam pairs) to obtain quantitative estimates of all the genetic sources of variation mentioned above. As an illustration of the estimation of heritability the example of the regression of offspring on one parent will be considered. Suppose the phenotypic values for a particular character are available on a group of individuals and on each of their female parents and the relationship between offspring and parent is known. From these paired observations it is possible to calculate the regression coefficient of offspring on parent, b_{OP}.

Now, $$b_{OP} = \frac{\text{covariance offspring and parent}}{\text{variance of parents}}$$

The variance of parents is equal to the phenotypic variance σ_P^2. What does the covariance represent in genetic terms? To answer this question it is necessary to return to the single locus situation. It is important to realize in what follows that the mean genotypic value of an offspring is by definition half the breeding value of one parent. The required values are given in the following table:

Parents		Expressed as deviations from population mean		
Genotype	Frequency	Parents genotypic value	Parents breeding value	Offspring mean genotypic value
JJ	p^2	$2q(a-pd)$	$2q[a+d(q-p)]$	$q[a+d(q-p)]$
Jj	$2pq$	$a(q-p) + d(1-2pq)$	$(q-p)[a+d(q-p)]$	$\frac{1}{2}(q-p)[a+d(q-p)]$
jj	q^2	$-2p(a+qd)$	$-2p[a+d(q-p)]$	$-p[a+d(q-p)]$

Thus the covariance of offspring and parent genotypic values

$$= \Sigma \left(\text{Frequency} \times \left\{ \begin{array}{c} \text{parent genotypic value} \\ \text{as deviation from mean} \end{array} \right\} \times \left\{ \begin{array}{c} \text{offspring genotypic value} \\ \text{as deviation from mean} \end{array} \right\} \right)$$

$$= p^2\{2q(a - pd)\}\{q[a + d(q - p)]\} + 2pq\{a(q - p) + d(1 - 2pq)\}$$
$$\{\tfrac{1}{2}(q - p)[a + d(q - p)]\} + q^2\{ - 2p(a + qd)\}\{ - p[a + d(q - p)]\}$$

This reduces to, $pq[a + d(q - p)]^2$, which represents half the variance of breeding values or $\tfrac{1}{2}\sigma_A^2$.

So
$$b_{OP} = \frac{\tfrac{1}{2}\sigma_A^2}{\sigma_P^2}$$

Therefore
$$2b_{OP} = h^2$$

The two most commonly used methods of estimating heritability are by calculating the variance of half sib or full sib family means. The variance of half sib family means, σ_{HS}^2, can be shown to equal $\tfrac{1}{4}\sigma_A^2$ whilst the variance of full sib family means, σ_{FS}^2, equals $\tfrac{1}{2}\sigma_A^2 + \tfrac{1}{4}\sigma_D^2$.

Thus
$$\frac{4\sigma_{HS}^2}{\sigma_P^2} = \frac{\sigma_A^2}{\sigma_P^2} = h^2$$

and
$$\frac{2\sigma_{FS}^2}{\sigma_P^2} = \frac{\sigma_A^2 + \tfrac{1}{2}\sigma_D^2}{\sigma_P^2} = h^2 + \frac{\tfrac{1}{2}\sigma_D^2}{\sigma_P^2}$$

The estimate derived from full sib family means is likely to be an overestimate because it contains half the dominance variance in addition to the additive genetic variance. All the methods which have been mentioned are likely to be overestimates in some degree because the numerators in each case contain different proportions of the interaction variance, σ_I^2. The estimate from full sibs is biased upwards by any common maternal effects within the full sib families and the estimate from the parent-offspring regression, particularly the dam-daughter regression, is similarly biased by common maternal and environmental effects between paired individuals of the two generations. The half sib family estimate is expected to be the least biased because common environmental effects within half sib families are rather less likely than for the other relationships. The offspring-sire regression is not likely to be biased by common environmental effects between generations but contains twice the proportion of the interaction variance contained in the estimate from half sibs. These qualifications have been mentioned to stress the point that figures quoted for the heritability of a character are estimates subject to error, and dependent on the method of calculation.

Table 2 Comparisons of heritability calculated by different methods from the same source data – the characters are of body weight and gain at several ages in breeds of sheep. (BOWMAN. 1968 in *Growth and Development of Mammals*, edited by Lodge, G.A. and Lamming, G.E., London, Butterworth, 291–308)

Reference	Character	Method of calculating heritability*				
		FS	HS	OD	OS	OMP
Botkin (1964)	Weaning wt.	0.59	0.21			
	Initial wt. on test	0.68	0.24			
	Final wt. on test	0.56	0.20			
	Gain from weaning to end of test	0.32	0.08			
	Gain on test	0.24	0.12			
Carter and McClure (1962)	Gain from birth to weaning		0.02		0.03	
	120 day wt.		0.12		0.08	
Ensminger et al. (1943)	Shropshire birth wt.		0.10	0.10		
	Shropshire 140 day wt.		0.12	0.12		
	Southdown birth wt.		0.08	0.40		
	Southdown 140 day wt.		0.12	0.06		
Hazel and Terrill (1946)	Corriedale weaning wt.		0.32	0.45		
	Targhee weaning wt.		0.08	−0.01		
	Columbia weaning wt.		0.16	0.21		
Hazel and Terrill (1945)	Ramboillet weaning wt.		0.27±0.05	0.34±0.08		
Nelson and Venkatachalam (1949)	Birth wt.		0.29±0.14	0.72±0.10		
	Weaning wt.		0.42±0.21	0.15±0.17		
Warwick and Cartwright (1957)	120 day wt.		0.56	0.77	0.27	0.41
Yao et al. (1953)	Birth wt.		0.18	0.35		0.25

FS=full sib. HS=half sibs. OD=offspring-dam. OS=Offspring-sire. OMP=offspring-midparent.

An illustration of the differences in value of heritability calculated by different methods from the same source data is given in Table 2. In the examples quoted, heritability has been calculated by several authors for various weight and growth characters in sheep. The half sib estimates are lower than the full sib estimates indicating that dominance variance, σ_D^2, probably represent an important part of the total variance. With one exception the estimates from offspring dam regression are similar to or larger than the estimates from half sibs. Those cases which are larger can be explained by important common maternal and environmental effects between the offspring dam pairs. Where possible, it is advisable to use the half sib estimate, which is the least biased estimate of h^2.

Apart from the method of calculation, it must be stressed that heritability estimates are specific to the generation and population of which the data, from which they were derived, came. In part this point is illustrated in Table 3. Heritability of body weight at a specific age in cattle has been calculated by many workers for different breeds. Included in the table are the number of animals recorded to obtain the estimate. Generally the more data, the more reliable the estimate. The heritabilities reported range from nearly 0 to 1 and the problem is to know which of the estimates is reliable. The extreme values tend to be based on comparatively few records and estimates based on less than 300 animals can be given little emphasis. Most of the estimates are in the region of 0.4 to 0.8 so that as a generalization it is said that the heritability of body weight at maturity in cattle is approximately 0.7. However, it should also be

Table 3 Heritability estimates of final weight of cattle after performance test. (After PRESTON & WILLIS, 1974, *Intensive Beef Production*, Pergamon, Oxford.)

Location	No. of records	Breed	h^2	Authors
U.K.	986	F	0.12[a,b]	Hodges *et al.*, 1961
Arkansas	179	A, H, S	0.21	Gacula & Brown, 1963
U.K.	911	RP, DS	0.27[a,b]	Mason, 1964
Israel	1563	F	0.33[b]	Soller *et al.*, 1966a,b
S. Dakota	336	H	0.33[c]	Wilson *et al.*, 1962
Germany	525	F	0.40[b]	Langlet, 1965
California	200	H	0.41	Rollins *et al.*, 1962
S. Dakota	473	H	0.45	Wilson *et al.*, 1963[b]
Ohio	832	H	0.47	Swiger *et al.*, 1961[b]
Nebraska	741	H	0.49[c]	Swiger *et al.*, 1961b
Montana	616	H	0.55	Shelby *et al.*, 1963
Montana	616	H	0.64	Shelby *et al.*, 1963
Germany	418	Simmental	0.65[d]	Averdunk., 1968
New Mexico	499	H	0.70	Blackwell *et al.*, 1962
Nebraska	480	A, H, S	0.72	Swiger *et al.*, 1965
Montana	542	H	0.77	Shelby *et al.*, 1960
New Mexico	499	H	0.77[b]	Blackwell *et al.*, 1962
Germany	418	Simmental	0.79[e]	Averdunk, 1968
Montana	635	H	0.84	Shelby *et al.*, 1955
Arkansas	371	A, H	0.85	Brown & Gacula, 1962
Montana	880	H	0.86	Knapp & Clark, 1950
Texas	241	Various	1.00	Dubose & Cartwright, 1967
Preferred value			0.70	

[a]On grass. [b]Weight per day of age. [c]Adjusted to the same age. [d]420 days. [e]364 days. A = Angus. DS = Dairy Shorthorn. F = Friesan. H = Hereford. RP = Red Poll. S = Shorthorn.

noted that there are reliable and marked differences in heritability for this character between breeds. As an estimate of heritability is needed in order to plan breeding programmes effectively it is advisable, in the absence of a reliable estimate from the specific population on which the breeding programme is to be carried out, to take an estimate which has been calculated on data on the same breed and if possible from the same geographical area. For instance, the heritability of body weight in Herefords in the United Kingdom may differ from that in the United States because of the genetic separation of the two populations over a period of several generations, and because the two populations may have been subject to different selection practices.

A range of heritability values for different characters in domesticated species is given in Table 4. It can be seen that those characters closely associated with

Table 4 Heritabilities of characters in several domesticated species (approximate values from several estimates in each case).

Species	Character	Heritability
Cattle	Birth weight	0.40
	Weaning weight	0.35
	Mature weight	0.70
	Calving interval	0.05
	Milk yield	0.04
	Butterfat yield	0.30
Sheep	Birth weight	0.10–0.35
	Weaning weight	0.10–0.40
	Mature weight	0.20–0.40
	Clean fleece yield	0.45
	Litter size	0.10
Pigs	Birth weight	0.15
	Mature weight	0.25
	Litter size at birth	0.15
Chicken	Annual survivor egg production	0.20
	Egg weight	0.60
	Body weight at 22 weeks	0.25
Turkey	Body weight at 24 weeks	0.60
	Egg production	0.15
	Fertility	0.20
	Hatchability	0.15
Buffalo	Mature weight	0.30–0.50
	Milk yield	0.20–0.30
Horse	Body weight	0.25–0.30
	Draught power	0.25
	Racing ability	0.35
Goat	Litter size	0.10–0.25
	Milk yield	0.20–0.30

reproduction and survival of the young have low heritabilities, and that the values tend to get larger for characters like adult weight, carcase traits and morphological characters. In general the more closely a character affects the fitness of an individual to reproduce the lower the heritability is likely to be. It is assumed that natural selection has eliminated all but the most suitable genotypes for characters of reproductive fitness with the result that there is practically no additive genetic variation left. This statement should not be taken to imply that all genetic variation for these characters has been eliminated because there is evidence that non-additive and epistatic variation of a complex type still exists, but this is difficult to modify directionally by selection.

In conclusion, it should be clear that the term heritability is used to define the additive genetic proportion of the phenotypic variance. The estimates of this proportion vary by reason of the amount and source of data involved, the method of calculation and the character and species concerned. Heritability estimates are required in order to plan and excute selection programmes. If the estimates are zero, then there is no additive genetic variation and certain forms of selection will be ineffective and should not be attempted. In these circumstances, it is then useful to obtain estimates of the dominance and interaction variances. If they prove to be positive then there are forms of selection which can be applied to exploit these non-additive sources of genetic variation. If there is no genetic variation at all, selection will be totally ineffective. The estimation of the phenotypic variance and its subdivision into its genetic and environmental components, including the calculation of heritability, is the essential first step in deciding whether to select and the form of selection to apply for the improvement of a quantitative character.

4 Selection for a Single Character

4.1 Selection in theory

In breeding animals whose population size is not declining more gametes and offspring are produced than are required to maintain the population. Throughout the life cycle surplus gametes and offspring are discarded and do not contribute any genetic material to the next generation and the maintenance of the population. The determination of which gametes and which offspring shall survive and of the number of gametes and offspring which each chosen parent shall produce is the process of selection. Where the choice is determined by the suitability of the characteristics of the gamete or individual for survival in the environment in which they must exist, then it is called natural selection. Where the choice is determined by actions of man in choosing animals as parents which most closely meet his requirements, whether they be economic or pleasure objectives, then it is called artificial selection. The distinction is important because the two forms of selection may be complementary or antagonistic but rarely if ever unrelated. For example, artificial selection of individuals as parents which produce many offspring is complementary to the survival of the population, whereas artificial selection of individuals as parents which have low body weight which may impair their survival is antagonistic to natural selection. Similarly artificial selection for small litter size, which reduces the opportunity for future selection and decreases the chances of survival of the population, is likely to be antagonistic to natural selection. Thus both the character and the direction of artificial selection determine the relationship between it and natural selection. Artificial selection is applied at some stage post parturition or hatching and up to any time after sexual maturity, whereas natural selection is operating throughout the life cycle of the species. In consequence in those cases where the two forms of selection are antagonistic natural selection will at least partially negate the efforts of the breeder.

The purpose of artificial selection is to change over a period of several generations the gene frequency in a population so that the genotypes produced are those most closely meeting the requirements of the breeder. The first essential in establishing a selection programme is to define the objective, which is usually much more difficult to do than it may seem. This is because at the outset the type of individual required in large numbers may not exist at all in the foundation population for the programme and therefore must be an abstract target for which the breeder is aiming, and because it may be difficult to define the objective in precise quantitative terms, which can easily be measured and recorded. For instance, the breeder may decide that he requires larger cattle.

Then it is necessary to ascertain whether he requires heavier cattle or whether they should be taller or longer, whether it matters if the increase is achieved as a consequence of changes in body composition such as a higher proportion of fat and less muscle and bone and so on. In fact, an enquiry of this kind may lead to the discovery that the breeder has defined his true needs very imprecisely. In the example mentioned it may become clear that the breeder did not really need larger cattle but that he needed cattle producing a higher proportion of muscle (lean meat) in the carcase. Some objectives are very much easier to define than others and the choice of objectives and criteria on which to base selection will determine the ease, efficiency and cost of the selection programme.

Having established the objective, the next step is to determine the measurement to be recorded on all individuals in the population, which will be used as the criterion for selection. In many cases the measurement may coincide with the terms of the objective but in many others the measurement used for selection purposes is an indirect assessment of the objective. Thus if heavier cattle are required, the animals can be weighed easily and relatively accurately. However, if an animal is required which produces more lean meat then the measurement has to be an indirect one because the body composition cannot be determined directly until the animal has been slaughtered. Then the selection criterion might be the weight of the animal coupled with some assessment of fat over the longissimus dorsi muscle which can be determined in live animals by means of an ultrasonic device. The principles which govern the choice of selection criteria may be summarized as follows:

(*i*)   Closely related to the objective.
(*ii*)   Easily, quickly, accurately and cheaply measured.
(*iii*) Capable of being measured early in life, preferably before sexual maturity, and preferably in both sexes.

Artificial selection is the choice of some individuals from among a larger number of individuals to be parents of the next generation. All potential parents have to be recorded for the criterion of selection and the required number of individuals most closely meeting the breeder's objectives are selected. The difference between the mean performance of the selected individuals, P_s, and the mean of the population before selection, P_u, is termed the *selection differential*, S, and may be considered the attempted gain which the breeder is trying to achieve towards his objective. If, as is usual, it is assumed that the character in the population under selection is distributed according to the normal distribution then there is a useful relationship between the proportion selected and the selection differential. By dividing the selection differential by the phenotypic standard deviation the *standardized selection differential* or *selection intensity*, i, is obtained.

Thus
$$i = \frac{\bar{P}_s - \bar{P}_u}{\sigma_P}$$

For the normal distribution there is a relationship between the deviation, in standard deviation units, from the mean and the proportion of individuals having values exceeding such a deviation (see HEATH, 1970). In fact it can be shown that the average deviation from the mean, in units of σ_P, of a proportion, p, of individuals with extreme values above or below the mean is z/p, where z is the height of the ordinate at the point of truncation of a proportion, p, of the population. During selection, it is normal to select individuals which deviate from the mean in one direction only and appropriate tables are available for the average deviation in units of standard deviation for a selected proportion of one tail of the distribution. Then it can be seen that the selection intensity $i=S/\sigma_P=z/p$. These various parameters are illustrated in Fig. 4–1.

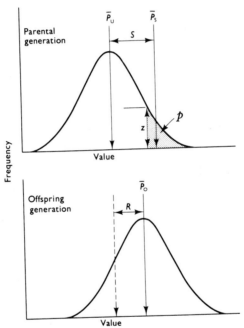

Fig. 4–1   The effect of selection, for definition of symbols see text.

Remembering that heritability is the regression of breeding value on phenotypic value and that the genotypic value of an offspring is half the sum of the breeding values of its two parents, then the genotypic value, and therefore the phenotypic value, $\bar{P}_o$, of the offspring can be predicted from the product of the mean phenotypic value of the parents and the heritability. If it is assumed that there is no environmental change between one generation and the next then the predicted value,

$$\bar{P}_o = (\bar{P}_s - \bar{P}_u)h^2 + \bar{P}_u$$

or the predicted genetic gain, ΔG, for a generation as a consequence of selection can be stated as $\Delta G = \bar{P}_o - \bar{P}_u = (\bar{P}_s - \bar{P}_u)h^2 = Sh^2 = i\sigma_P h^2$. Thus knowing the heritability, the standard deviation, and choosing any stated proportion of the population as selected parents, it is possible to predict the mean phenotypic value of the following generation. In practice, if a selection programme is carried out then the actual genetic gain or response R can be measured. Taking the actual response, the realized heritability can be calculated. By rearrangement of the formula above, it can be seen that

$$\text{Realized heritability, } h_R^2 = \frac{R}{i\sigma_P}$$

For various reasons, frequently the realized heritability is different, though not markedly so, from the value of the heritability obtained from data on the unselected population. One reason is that the estimate of the selection intensity from tables assumes that the parents chosen will contribute equal numbers of progeny to the next generation. In practice, because of the effects of natural selection, this rarely happens unless special precautions are taken to see that it does. Even then the precautions may fail because some selected parents are sterile. This source of discrepancy can be overcome if the selection intensity is calculated in the form of a *weighted selection differential* in which the deviations, from the unselected mean, of the selected parents are weighted according to their contribution to the offspring generation. A second reason is that random mating of the parents is assumed in deriving the heritability. In practice and as a consequence of selection prior to mating, parents of similar phenotype (phenotypic assortative mating) are mated together. A third reason is that selection, if effective, alters the population gene frequencies and genotypic values resulting from various forms of non-additive gene action. The prediction equation and heritability refer to changes in genotypic value resulting from gene frequency changes affecting additive genetic effects alone.

It will be noted that equations of response to selection refer to genetic gain per generation. The generation interval, t (the time in years between a specified stage in the life cycle of one generation and the same stage in the next generation), varies considerably between species and between different forms of selection programme. The breeder is usually interested in genetic gain per unit time so that the more useful form of measuring genetic change is from the equation

$$\Delta G \text{ per year} = \frac{i\sigma_P h^2}{t}$$

In all the important domesticated species, because of the differential reproductive rate between sexes, it is possible to apply a higher selection intensity to males than females. Thus with the use of artificial insemination it is possible to mate and produce calves from over 30 000 cows per year from a single bull; a cow will produce a single calf in the same time. Therefore of all the bull calves born, a very small proportion, perhaps 1 in 10 000, have to be saved to reproduce the population. By contrast between half and two-thirds of all heifer calves born have to be saved to maintain the population. Also the generation interval may be different between the sexes within a species depending on the age of reproduction determined by the selection programme. To take account of these variations, the prediction equation for genetic gain becomes

$$\Delta G \text{ per year} = \left(\frac{i_m + i_f}{t_m + t_f} \right) \sigma_P h^2$$

where i_m and i_f refer to the selection intensities for males and females respectively and t_m and t_f refer to the generation intervals for males and females respectively.

From the theoretical viewpoint, the equation indicates that the rate of genetic change can be altered by changing the heritability, the selection intensity and the generation interval separately or simultaneously. The possibility of increasing heritability by reducing environmental variation is slight and in any case would result in a simultaneous reduction in the standard deviation. The selection intensity can be increased by decreasing the proportion selected. This can be achieved either by selecting fewer parents or by recording more individuals and selecting parents from a larger group of potential parents. Selecting fewer parents leads to a greater rate of inbreeding, which as will be discussed later may be undesirable. The appropriate number of recorded individuals and selected parents will depend on the individual breeder's judgement of the facilities he has available for keeping and recording animals, on the rate of inbreeding (determined by parental population size) which he is prepared to accept in his animals and on the selection intensity to be applied to optimize genetic gain. There are possibilities for reducing generation interval but the breeder frequently runs into conflicts between reducing generation interval and attempts to increase selection intensity. In order to have more individuals available to record as potential parents and so increase selection intensity it may be necessary to extend the generation interval. There is no simple way of determining the appropriate choice of population size, selection intensity and generation interval and each potential design must be tested in the equations above to predict its potential for rate of gain. Some examples of alternative designs for selection of eight-week weight in chickens are given in Table 5. The greatest rate of genetic gain is predicted from a design with a population size of either 500 or 1250 males and females and a selection intensity of 1 in 50 for males and 1 in 5 for females. Higher selection intensity does not lead to greater response because the generation interval is greatly increased.

Table 5 The predicted genetic gain from some alternative programmes for the selection of body weight at 8 weeks in chickens.

Number of unselected parents		Number of selected parents		i in units of σ_P		t in weeks	σ_P in g	h^2	$\Delta G/t$ in g/week
♂	♀	♂	♀	♂	♀	♂ and ♀			
500	500	2	20	2.962	2.154	53	100	0.4	1.93
500	500	10	100	2.421	1.400	33	100	0.4	2.32
500	500	25	250	2.063	0.798	30	100	0.4	1.91
1000	1000	25	250	2.338	1.271	32	100	0.4	2.26
1250	1250	25	250	2.421	1.400	33	100	0.4	2.32

Under natural mating, a ratio of one male to ten females is usual. It is assumed that the first offspring are hatched when the hen is 28 weeks old and that thereafter approximately two live offspring per week are produced. The sex ratio of offspring is assumed to be 1♂ : 1♀. Selection is of those offspring which are heaviest at 8 weeks of age and is carried out separately within sexes.

The prediction equation for genetic gain refers to a single generation of selection. If selection is effective, one consequence, as we have seen, is to change gene frequency in the population. The additive genetic variance and the heritability are a function of gene frequency. Selection will therefore change heritability and the direction and magnitude of change will depend on the gene frequencies in the base population. In the absence of dominance, if the frequencies of the desired genes are less than 0.5 and then decline until heritability is zero when loci carrying the required genes are homozygous. In most cases of selection in practice the frequency of desirable genes affecting important economic characters is assumed to be greater than 0.5. To what extent is it necessary, in order to predict genetic gain in a selection programme, to obtain a revised estimate of heritability each generation? From observation of selection experiments with both laboratory and farm animals the conclusion is, that the amount of change per generation of gene frequency and of heritability is usually so small, that an initial estimate of heritability can be used for a prediction of genetic gain for between five and ten generations of selection before a revised estimate becomes essential. However, it must be stressed that as heritability declines the genetic gain per unit of selection applied declines and when heritability becomes very small the response may not justify the effort. This becomes an economic problem which will be explored in more detail later.

4.2 Selection in practice

Reference to a selection programme for high and low eight-week body weight in chickens carried out by SIEGEL (1962) illustrates the results and parameters obtained. A population of White Plymouth Rocks, developed at the Virginia Agricultural Station, was used as the base population. From it, two selection lines were developed by taking the heaviest individuals at eight weeks of age as parents of one line (the H line) and the lightest individuals at the same age as parents of the other line (the L line). Thereafter, within each line, 8 males and 48 females were selected as parents each generation. Mating of selected individuals within a line, in groups of 6 females to 1 male, was at random, except that matings of half sibs or more closely related individuals were prevented. The offspring for each generation were produced from two hatches in consecutive weeks and were reared in floor pens under as similar conditions of nutrition, temperature, humidity and lighting as possible. In this way the environmental differences between generations were minimized. The programme was continued for four cycles of selection.

The numbers of offspring recorded in each generation together with their mean weights are given in Table 6. The means of unselected and selected males and females for each generation are shown in Fig. 4–2. Several typical features of selection are illustrated by these results.

Table 6 Means and number of chicks by sex, line and generation for body weight at 8 weeks of age. (From SIEGEL. 1962, *Poultry Science*, **41**, 954–62.)

Item	Sex	Line[1]	P_1	F_1	F_2	F_3	F_4
					Generation		
No. of individuals	♂	H	249	234	187	185	169
	♂	L	249	214	146	218	213
	♀	H	250	194	167	198	137
	♀	L	250	193	140	214	203
Means±standard deviations (g)	♂	H	879±123	944±120	946±158	1038±105	1156±114
	♂	L		868±113	746±152	755±104	835± 98
		H–L		76**	200**	283**	321**
	♀	H	715±117	775±100	777±141	833± 87	951± 98
	♀	L		705± 94	588±132	615±104	652±112
		H–L		70**	189**	218**	294**

** $P \leq 0.01$
[1] H=High weight line; L=Low weight line.

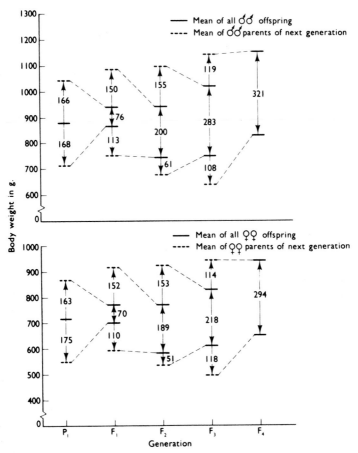

Fig. 4–2 Mean eight-week body weights for unselected male and female offspring and for the parents of the next generation, in each generation of the high and low weight lines, showing the effects of selection. (From SIEGEL, 1962, *Poultry Science*, **41**, 954–62.)

Firstly the number of offspring available for selection is not the same from generation to generation even though the number of parents is equal. This represents variation in reproduction of parents and viability of embryos and offspring. Consequently there is variation in the selection differential applied for each sex both between generations within a line and between lines within a generation. Since the selection differential varies it is hardly surprising that the response is variable between sexes, lines and generations. If individual lines are examined, the high line males are found to have changed by +65, +2, +92 and +118 g respectively in the four generations of selection. The low line males have changed by −11, −122, +9 and +80 g respectively in the four generations. Thus in spite of selection for low body weight, comparison of generation means for individual lines indicates that the males of this line increased in weight in two generations. Over the four generations of selection the low line males decreased from a mean of 879 g to 835 g. In addition to the variation in selection applied there are two other more important reasons for the variation in response, indeed for the apparent negative response in some generations. One is that in the size of population used in this experiment and for a quantitative character controlled by many loci the probability of all possible genotypes occurring is low. In some generations the required genotypes may not be represented. The selection theory is based on the assumption that random mating and large population size will permit the presence and selection of desired genotypes. Therefore the effect of restricted population size is to allow only a sample of possible genotypes in expected frequencies to exist each generation and the sampling effect leads to variation in response, between generations and from the predicted values. The other reason is that even though every effort was made to standardize the environment throughout the four generations, environmental fluctuations would occur. For instance, the poultryman, who can have a marked effect on livestock performance, may be changed between generations, the exposure to disease might change and there are many other sources of environmental variation which were not controlled. In some generations these environmental fluctuations will cause heavier birds and in other generations lighter birds. Therefore the change in mean performance of a single population is the combined result of changes caused by selection and those caused by random environmental effects. In order to measure the effect of selection alone it is necessary to separate the genetic and environmental changes. If it is assumed that at any point in time the environment will affect equally the birds in the high and low weight lines then the difference between the two lines is solely the genetic difference between them resulting from the combined selection applied in opposite directions. The difference in mean between the lines for male weights increases from 76 g in generation 1 to 200, 283 and 321 g in generations 2, 3 and 4 respectively. Similarly female weights between the lines diverge by 70, 189, 218 and 294 g for the four generations. Thus there is a marked increase in the divergence between the weights within sexes for the two selection lines.

Except in the F_2 generation for the low line, the number of offspring hatched and recorded, enabled similar selection pressures to be applied to the high and low lines within generations. The expected selection differentials are given in Table 7. These have been calculated from the unweighted parental deviations. The effective selection differentials, in which the parental deviations were weighted according to the number of offspring they produced to contribute to the mean of the following generation, are also given. The expected selection differential is the effect of artificial selection, whereas the effective selection differential is the effect of the artificial selection as modified by natural selection. A comparison of expected and effective selection differentials indicates the extent to which natural selection operates on the character being artificially selected. The ratios of effective to expected selection differentials shown in Table 7 indicate that natural selection was largely unimportant in affecting the response to selection for eight-week body weight. In generation F_3 the ratio of 1.37 for male selection in the low weight line gives some support for the view that natural selection favours low body weight but the evidence is not strong as most of the ratios are close to 1.0.

Table 7   Comparison of effective and expected selection differentials by generation.[1] (From SIEGEL, 1962, *Poultry Science*, **41**, 954–62.)

| Selection[2] differential | Line | Parents of offspring in | | | |
		F_1	F_2	F_3	F_4
Expected	H	+164.0	+144.4	+163.0	+117.6
	L	−179.9	−108.8	− 44.7	−119.6
	H–L	343.9	253.2	207.7	237.2
Effective	H	+165.5	+150.5	+155.3	+119.2
(♂ offspring)	L	−168.5	−112.5	− 61.4	−107.8
	H–L	334.0	263.0	216.7	227.0
Effective	H	+162.7	+152.0	+153.3	+113.9
(♀ offspring)	L	−174.8	−110.3	− 50.6	−118.5
	H–L	337.5	262.3	203.9	232.4
Effective ÷ expected	H	1.01	1.04	0.95	1.01
(♂ offspring)	L	0.94	1.03	1.37	0.90
	H–L	0.97	1.04	1.04	0.96
Effective ÷ expected	H	0.99	1.05	0.94	0.97
(♀ offspring)	L	0.97	1.01	1.13	0.99
	H–L	0.98	1.04	0.98	0.98

[1] Effective selection differential – each parent's deviation was weighted according to the number of offspring used in computing the mean for the line and generation.

[2] Expected selection differential – unweighted parental deviations.

[3] The mean increase (+) and decrease (−) in 8-week body weight of selected parents, compared with the unselected offspring in the same line the preceding generation.

The estimates of heritability for sexes and generations separately are shown in Table 8. The realized heritability has been calculated as the mean difference between unselected progeny of the two lines divided by the total amount of selection applied to achieve the difference. The other or predictive heritability estimates have been calculated from the offspring-on-dam regression. The realized heritabilities are fairly consistent and give no indication of decreasing as a consequence of selection. They are also similar but lower except in the F_1 generation than the predictive estimates. The offspring-on-dam regression estimates are more variable and there is no obvious explanation for the very low estimates for the F_1 generation or for the steady rise in the estimates for females from the F_1 to the F_4 generation. They were calculated from fewer than 240 pairs of observations in each case so that the standard estimates are large. The selection programme indicates that in this population the heritability of eight-week body weight is approximately 0.3.

This example illustrates the practice and results of a simple mass selection programme for a single, easily measured, character. It also illustrates the sort of variation in response which is found and indicates how the genetic response can be distinguished from the total generation change resulting from genetic and environmental sources.

4.3 Population size and random drift

Reference has already been made to the effect of finite population size on genotypic and gene frequency as a possible cause of divergence between actual and predicted response in a selection programme. This effect requires some elaboration as it has important implications for the design and expected response of selection programmes. In a large random mating population in the idealized state, the theory of the Hardy-Weinburg equilibrium indicates that in each generation gene frequency will stay constant. If, however, an idealized population is of finite size involving N parents in the first generation, then the following generations will be composed of N parents which have come from $2N$ gametes produced by the first generation parents. The $2N$ gametes which compose the second generation parents are a random sample of the total and excessive number of gametes produced by the first generation parents and of the total offspring population from which the second generation parents were randomly chosen.

Table 8   Heritability estimates by sex and generation for body weight at 8 weeks of age (from SIEGEL, 1962, *Poultry Science*, **41**, 954-62).

Method of computation	Sex	Generation				Unweighted means
		F_1	F_2	F_3	F_4	
Realized	♂	0.23	0.33	0.35	0.31	0.30
	♀	0.21	0.32	0.27	0.28	0.27
	combined	0.22	0.32	0.31	0.30	0.29
Offspring-dam regression within sire	♂	−0.15	0.36	0.35	0.32	0.22
	♀	0.04	0.39	0.42	0.59	0.36
	combined	−0.06	0.38	0.38	0.46	0.29

Thus in the case of a finite population, the expectation is that its gene frequency in each generation will be constant but because of the sampling effect the actual gene frequency may vary. How much is it expected to vary? If the gene frequencies of a pair of alleles in the first generation of a population of size N are p_1 and q_1, the change in gene frequency which occurs from one generation to the next can be designated Δq. If from the first generation replicated second generations (sub-populations), each of size N, are produced then the variance of Δq between these sub-populations is

$$\sigma^2_{\Delta q} = \frac{p_1 q_1}{2N}$$

If the process is repeated from the second to the third generations, the expectation is that the average gene frequency, $\bar{q}$, of all the sub-populations will still be q_1, but because each second generation sub-population had a different gene frequency, the frequencies in the third generation will vary still more. After t generations the variance of gene frequencies among the populations can be shown to be

$$\sigma^2_q = p_1 q_1 \left[1 - \left(1 - \frac{1}{2N}\right)^t\right]$$

The smaller the sub-population size the greater the variance of gene frequency between the sub-populations in any generation. Starting from a single population and producing several generations of sub-populations leads, even in the absence of selection, to a divergence of the gene frequency in the separate sub-populations. This process is called random drift. In addition to the variation of gene frequencies, there is a change in genotypic frequencies within the separate sub-populations and in the population as a whole. In both there is a decrease in the frequency of heterozygotes and an increase in the frequency of homozygotes. The redistribution of genotypic frequencies can be quantified as:

Genotype	Frequency in whole population
JJ	$p_1^2 + \sigma^2_q$
Jj	$2p_1 q_1 - q2\sigma^2_q$
jj	$q_1^2 + \sigma^2_q$

Eventually and theoretically all sub-populations will be completely homozygous and then the expectation is that in the whole population the proportion of sub-populations which are homozygous JJ is p_1 and the proportion of sub-populations which are homozygous jj is q_1. Thus the effects of finite population size are a random drift of gene frequency with an eventual drift to complete homozygosity, and in consequence a loss of genetic variation. Therefore the breeder attempts to make the number of selected parents large so that he loses little genetic variation as a result of random drift and as much as possible as a result of his artificial selection.

4.4 Measurement of genetic change

Only in the experimental situation would it be economically justifiable to measure genetic response by selecting two populations, one each in opposite directions. One of the populations is always likely to be commercially uneconomic. Nevertheless, it is vital for the animal breeder to have some way of ascertaining to what extent the selection he applies leads to genetic response. He must not assume that because he applies selection he obtains response. There are several alternative ways by which genetic response can be measured separately, from the overall change in performance. One effective method now widely used by poultry and pig breeders is the use of genetic control populations. The theory is that in the same contemporaneous environment, an unselected control population is maintained and reproduced at the same time as the population under selection. Assuming that the changes in the environment have equivalent effects on the performance of the control and selected populations and assuming that it is possible to reproduce the control population in such a way that it stays genetically constant between generations, then changes in the performance of the control population will be of enviromental origin whereas those in the selected population will be both genetic and environmental. The difference in change between the two populations represents the genetic change in the selected population. One control population can be used to monitor the genetic change in several selected populations. Several designs have been suggested for the size, mating and reproduction of control populations. The important principles are designed to minimize changes in gene frequency caused by random drift and natural selection. The population size should be as large as facilities allow and the sex ratio should be close to $1\,\male:1\,\female$. The population size should be maintained constant from generation to generation, selection of any kind should be avoided and mating should be at random. The population should be reproduced so that each male parent contributes at random one male offspring and each female parent contributes at random one female offspring to the following generation.

An example of how a genetic control can be used to interpret the effect of selection is shown by some results of a poultry selection programme by GOWE and co-workers (1959) in Canada. They selected two populations (called the Ottawa and New strains) for increased egg production though some selection was applied for viability during rearing, fertility and hatchability as well. Results for five years of selection are available. A pedigree random-bred control population derived from the same population as the Ottawa selected population was maintained contemporaneously. The selected and control lines were tested at the same five farms each year. The results for hen housed production (the number of eggs laid in 500 days divided by the number of birds put into the laying houses) are shown in Fig. 4–3. The performance of the Ottawa and New lines increased by an average of 3.71 and 12.88 eggs per bird per year respectively, as indicated by the regression of actual performance on time. However, over the same period the control line increased by an average of 2.45 eggs per bird per year, and this is the effect of the changes in the environment. If the control is used as the base line to measure genetic change, then the Ottawa line increased by 1.26 and the New line by 7.30 eggs per bird

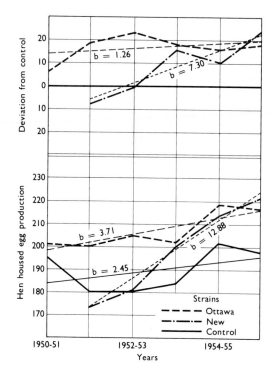

Fig. 4–3 Mean hen housed production over 6 years for three strains. Pooled data from five test farms. Production shown as the actual data and as a deviation from control performance. (From GOWE *et al.*, 1959, *Poultry Science*, **38**, 443–62.)

per year. Unless a control had been used the estimate of genetic change would have been considerably overestimated.

4.5 Long-term effects of selection

Some explanation has been made already about the causes of discrepancy between the actual response to selection and that predicted from heritability, phenotypic standard deviation and selection intensity. If several replicated populations (or lines) of the same size are started from the same base population and each is selected in identical manner, then the responses which have been observed in several experiments of this type are of the sort shown in Fig. 4–4. Some replicates reach their maximum response after a few generations, others respond more slowly and take many generations to reach their maximum performance and still others may hardly respond at all. The variation in response is related to replicate population size and is maximal for a population of 2 and is very small for populations of 100 parents and more. Eventually, in spite of continued selection, response ceases in all the replicates and at this level of performance the lines are said to have reached *selection plateaux*. It is assumed that because of artificial selection and random drift the lines are homozygous and additive genetic variation has been exhausted at those loci affecting the character under selection. The highest selection plateau reached by any line is called the *selection limit*. The total genetic gain which is the difference between the performance of the base population and the selection limit is the total response which can be achieved by selection. The number of generations of selection which it takes to achieve half the total genetic response is called the half life of the selection programme. These terms are illustrated on the selection responses in Fig. 4–4.

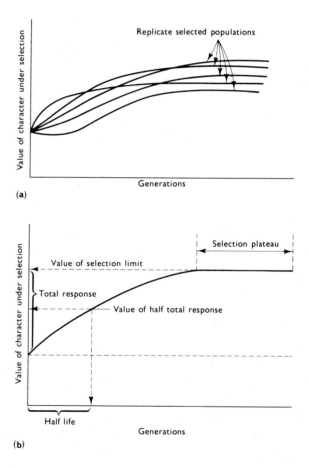

Fig. 4–4 The long-term response to selection. (**a**) The response obtained from replicate populations selected in exactly the same way. (**b**) definition of terms relating to the long-term effects of selection for a single selected population.

Theoretical studies by ROBERTSON (1960, *Proceedings of the Royal Society, B*, **153**, 234–49.) have shown some important relationships between the size of population, the intensity of selection and the selection limit, the total response and the half life of selection. Robertson reached the following conclusions:

(*i*)   'For a single gene with selective advantage *s*, the chance of fixation (the expected gene frequency at the limit) is a function only of *Ns*, where *N* is the effective population size. In artificial selection based on individual measurements, where the selection differential is *i* standard deviations, the expected limit of individual selection in any population is a function only of *Ni*.'

(*ii*) 'For low values of *Ni*, the total advance by selection is, for additive genes, 2*N* times the gain in the first generation but may be much greater than this for recessives, particularly if their initial frequency is low.'

(*iii*) 'The half life of any selection process will, for additive genes, not be greater than 1.4*N* generations but may, for rare recessives, equal 2*N*.'

(*iv*) 'In a selection programme of individual selection of equal intensity in both sexes, the furthest limit should be attained when half the population is selected from each generation.'

If a population reaches a selection plateau then the most likely way of achieving further response is by introducing genetic variation, for the character selected, to the population. This can be done by crossing the selected population with another population of different genetic origin but preferably one which has also been selected for the same character. Thus recombination of the best replicates at their selection limits might produce a population in which further response to selection could be gained, though combination of two populations selected for the same character but started from different base populations, in which different genes might be present, offers a better chance of continued genetic gain.

However, in considering a single base population, another important conclusion reached by Robertson is, that the selection limit of a population of size *N* parents is the same as the selection limit achieved by selecting *R* replicates each of population size *N/R* for several generations, combining them into one population of size *N* when each replicate has plateaued and finally selecting in the recombined population. On this basis there is no advantage in dividing a breeding population derived from one base population into selection replicates. However, the animal breeder is usually interested in short-term objectives and is unlikely to be making selection plans which only take into consideration the response to be achieved at the selection limit. He is much more likely to be interested in the genetic gain which can be achieved in the first 5 to 10 generations of selection. He has got to have some improved stock to sell to support his selection programme and thereafter changes in commercial requirements may force him to change his objectives. The practical problem in this situation is whether the expected performance of the best N/R replicates will exceed the expected performance of the population of size N in the early to middle generations of selection. Theoretical studies by BAKER and CURNOW (1969, *Crop Science*, **9**, 555–60.) suggest that there is expected to be an advantage in sub-dividing the population into replicates if the breeder wishes to maximize his gain after 10 or fewer generations. Some of their results when N is 256 and based on a model assuming 150 loci and additive gene action, are given in Table 9. For a population size of 64 and after ten generations of selection the best of four replicates (Total $N=4\times64=256$) had a mean of 99.6 compared to a mean of 97.8 for a single population of size 256 (which was the largest considered by Baker and Curnow). Even greater gain would be achieved by dividing the resources into more replicates, each of a smaller size. At the selection limit the largest single population had the highest expected mean.

The conclusions reached by Baker and Curnow were based on a model which contained only additive genetic variance. Results from computer simulations indicate there is good reason to expect that for characters for which there is substantial non-additive genetic variance (both dominance and epistasis), in addition to additive genetic variance, the advantages of replication in the early stages of selection will be even greater. However, if the maximum performance is to be obtained at the limit then none of the replicates should be discarded during selection. After some generations of selection, all the replicates should be recombined and selection pursued to the limit in a single large population. This is expected to lead to the same performance at the limit as selection in a single large population throughout. Selection between the replicates, in which some are discarded, is likely to lead to reduced performance at the selection limit. Replication of a large population by subdivision can be seen as a useful procedure for achieving more gain in the early stages of selection and in a way which may not jeopardize the performance at the selection limit.

Another consequence of the breeder being interested in short-term gains is that he is likely to use a selection intensity of less than 1 in 2, the selection intensity Robertson concluded to be optimal to maximize the selection limit. The higher selection intensity will produce greater initial genetic gain at the expense, which the breeder can afford, of a lower selection limit.

Confirmation that these theoretical predictions apply to selection programmes with animals are difficult to obtain. Very large populations and experimental facilities are required for the purpose and the time taken to reach selection limits is long particularly for the larger farm animals. Some results can be obtained more easily with laboratory animals than with farm species. For example ROBERTS (1966, *Genet. Res.*, **8**, 347–60) examined the results of several selection programmes for large and small body weight at 6 weeks of age in mice. One experiment of this sort is shown in Fig. 4–6. Roberts concluded from the results of several similar programmes that the limits attained do not stay stable over many generations and that in some cases, in spite of continued selection for high body weight, large lines having reached a generation peak may decrease in subsequent generations. The time taken to reach the limit for

Table 9 Expected genetic means, M, and standard deviations of genetic means, SD, for R replicate lines each with effective population size, N, after 1, 5, 10 and an infinite number of generations of selection. $NR = 256$. Additive genes. 150 loci. (Adapted from BAKER and CURNOW. 1969, *Crop Science*, **9**, 555–60, Table 5.)

| | | 1 generation | | | 5 generations | | | 10 generations | | | Infinite generations | | |
| | | All lines | | Best line | All lines | | Best line | All lines | | Best line | All lines | | Best line |
N	R	M	SD	M	M	SD	M	M	SD	M	M	SD	M
1	256	66.6	7.02	86.3	73.2	10.10	101.7	73.6	10.30	102.6	73.7	10.28	102.7
4	64	63.3	3.51	71.5	72.4	7.00	88.9	79.5	8.88	100.4	88.4	10.84	113.9
16	16	63.3	1.74	66.3	76.0	4.05	83.2	91.4	5.86	101.8	172.7	11.47	193.0
32	8	63.3	1.21	65.0	76.8	2.91	81.0	94.6	4.35	100.8	237.2	9.34	250.0
64	4	63.3	0.83	64.1	77.2	2.03	79.3	96.4	3.09	99.6	280.8	5.75	286.7
256	1	63.3	0.34	63.3	77.5	0.82	77.5	97.8	1.25	97.8	299.9	0.37	299.9

this trait varied between 10 and 30 generations which is a shorter time than is predicted by theory. Roberts estimated that genes at about 20 loci had contributed to the change in weight due to selection and concluded that the most likely cause for reaching a selection plateau was the exhaustion of additive genetic variance. Indeed relaxed or reversed selection in the large line in Fig. 4–5 failed to yield any response, thus supporting the conclusion that there was no remaining additive genetic variance. Relaxed or reversed selection in the small line in Fig. 4–5 did lead to some increase in body weight indict natural selection had prevented complete exhaustion of additive genetic variance for body weight.

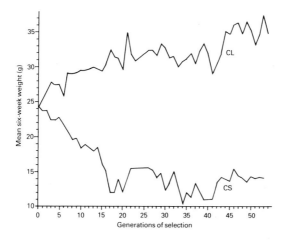

Fig. 4–5   An example of selection for high (CL) and low (CS) six week body weight in mice. Note the variability in generation means caused by environmental factors and by genetic changes. The differences between the lines represents the total genetic response to selection in opposite directions. The generation means are variable even at the selection limit. (From ROBERTS, 1966, *Genetical Research*, **8**, 361–75.)

5 Further Aspects of Selection

5.1 Various selection methods

In the previous chapter, the selection method described and exemplified by the programme of SIEGEL (1962) is called *individual or mass selection*. Essentially the procedure involves measuring or *performance testing* the potential parent individuals and then selecting as parents those with records closest to the objective. Individual selection is appropriate for characters with heritability in the range approximately 0.25–1.0 and which can easily be measured in the potential parents. For various reason this type of selection is not always the most appropriate and therefore in many cases other selection methods are used. The alternative methods involve making the selection on the basis of the performance of the relatives of the potential parents. The relatives are of three types, namely ancestors such as parents and grandparents, collateral relatives such as sibs, half sibs and cousins, and lastly progeny. Selection methods based on these three types of relatives are termed *pedigree selection, family selection* and *selection by progeny testing* respectively.

5.1.1 Pedigree selection

Pedigree refers to the recording of parentage so that the genetic relationships between individuals in a population are known. Such recording is required for all the selection methods to be discussed here. Only for individual or mass selection is it unnecessary to record pedigrees. For very many years breeders have based selection on the basis of parental and grandparental performance of potential parents. The expected genetic change per generation from pedigree selection using individual parental performances alone is, of course, half the change for individual selection for a comparable selection intensity, and slightly higher if grandparental performance is taken into account as well. There are certain circumstances, such as the inability to measure the character in one sex (e.g. milk yield), or characters which can only be measured relatively late in life (e.g. litter size in ewes), under which pedigree selection is more appropriate and efficient than individual selection. For characters which can only be measured in the female it is common practice to undertake an initial selection of males at a young age on the basis of female ancestor performance and later to supplement this with family selection or progeny testing. For characters which can only be measured late in life the generation interval for individual selection becomes very long and longer than for pedigree selection. Calculations show that then the rate of genetic change per unit time (*cf.* to per generation) is higher for pedigree than for individual selection and indeed for any other form of selection.

5.1.2 Family selection

By definition when the heritability of a character is in the range 0 to approximately 0.25 the phenotype of an individual is a relatively inaccurate estimate of its breeding value. Then it is more efficient in terms of genetic gain per unit time to base selection on family performance rather than on individual performance. For farm species large families of contemporary half sibs can be obtained easily, whereas full sib families contain few individuals which are usually not contemporaneous. Therefore the accuracy of the half sib family average is usually much higher than that for full sibs. Selection for characters of low heritability is usually achieved by choosing between groups of half sibs on the basis of their average performance, suitably weighted if the groups include different numbers of individuals.

There are two variations of family selection which are important in special situations. For characters for which there is a large proportion of environmental variation common to members within a family then *within family selection* becomes the appropriate method. Examples of this situation are the early growth and survival characters in pigs and lambs, where the sow and ewe provide a common maternal environment for each of their full sib families. Differences between families include not only genetic differences in growth and survival between progeny groups but also probably large genetic differences in maternal environment between female parents. If the aim is to improve early growth directly then selection between individuals within families should be practised, because between family selection would also improve maternal environment as measured by early growth but would not necessarily improve the genetic potential for early growth *per se* in the progeny. Obviously it is only possible to adopt within family selection for those species for which the family sharing the same maternal environment is large enough to allow a satisfactory selection intensity to be applied. Of the farm species this essentially means pigs.

The second variation of family selection is *sib selection*, and this is usually used by force of circumstances rather than by choice. For those characters which can be measured in only one sex or after an animal has been killed, such as various aspects of carcase quality, selection can be based on the performance of full or half sibs of the individuals used for breeding. The advent of artificial insemination and semen storage has made sib selection less necessary because if the male has to be killed to measure its performance, then semen can be collected from all potential male parents before slaughter and only that from selected males is used for inseminating selected females. However, sib selection is often used to improve carcase characters, particularly in pigs.

5.1.3 Selection by progeny testing

For characters of low heritability and again for characters which can only be measured in one sex or after slaughter, selection on the basis of progeny performance is appropriate, and more efficient than other forms of selection. Again because of the progeny group size which can be produced and recorded contemporaneously, the progeny test is usually on half sibs rather than full sibs alone. Selection by progeny testing is very similar to between family selection except that frequently the individuals which are measured to provide the progeny test are not those used for subsequent breeding. Thus a group of potential parents are mated and their progeny measured. Selection between the potential parents on the basis of progeny group averages, weighted to take account of different numbers of progeny, is followed by mating of the selected parents to produce a second batch of progeny. These are the next generation of potential parents which are then progeny tested. Artificial insemination has been invaluable in enabling progeny testing to be used extensively to improve dairy cattle especially, but also all the other major species except horses.

It should be emphasized that this is a brief description of the basic methods of selection which can be used depending on the nature of the character under selection. Combinations of these methods are also used and it is necessary to design the selection programme according to the objectives. In general, family selection or selection by progeny testing are most efficient for characters of low heritability, and individual selection for characters of medium to high heritability.

5.2 Correlated characters

So far selection has been described in terms of a single character. However, many characters are genetically correlated as a consequence of pleitropy and linkage. Therefore selection on one character leads to correlated changes in other characters. If the correlation is caused by pleiotropy there is no possibility of changing the relationship between the two characters. However, if linkage is the cause, then the relationship will alter when appropriate crossovers take place. The relationship can be quantified in the form of a genetic correlation, r_G, whose value is within the limits $+1$ to -1. This correlation can be estimated when two or more characters are measured on the types of individuals used for the estimation of heritability. From the value of the genetic correlation it is possible to predict the correlation changes which may occur in a second character as a consequence of selection on the primary character.

Thus $CR_2 = i_1 h_1 \sigma_{A2} r_G$ and $R_2 = i_2 h_2 \sigma_{A2}$

where CR_2 = indirect (correlated) response in character 2 as a result of selection on character 1

R_2 = direct response in character 2 to selection for character 2
h_1^2 and h_2^2 = heritability of characters 1 and 2 respectively
r_G = genetic correlation between characters 1 and 2
σ_{A2}^2 = additive genetic variance for character 2
i_1 and i_2 = selection intensity for characters 1 and 2 respectively

There are certain situations where greater response for a character can be achieved by selection for a correlated character than for the character itself.

Now
$$\frac{CR_2}{R_2} = \frac{i_1 h_1 \sigma_{A2} r_G}{i_2 h_2 \sigma_{A2}}$$

Assuming equal intensity of selection for each character the correlated response will be greater when $h_1 r_G$ exceeds h_2.

The use of correlated response is also valuable if the required character is very difficult or expensive to measure or when it can only be measured late in life causing very long generation intervals. For example it is expensive to accommodate, and to measure the individual feed intake of, animals to estimate their feed conversion. In most species growth rate is highly correlated ($r_G = 0.6$–0.8) with feed conversion so that selection for the latter is usually based on growth rate. However, a word of caution about the predictive value of genetic correlations should be entered here. Not only are their estimates subject to much more error than heritabilities for the same amount of data but they change more rapidly as a consequence of relatively small changes of gene frequency. Therefore the prediction of correlated responses from a one-generation estimate of a genetic correlation is likely to be valid for few, perhaps only two or three, generations ahead. Certainly the predictive value of a genetic correlation is less than of a heritability estimate.

Some impression of the correlated responses to be observed in selection programmes can be gained by further consideration of the experiment of SIEGEL (1962) referred to in Chapter 4. In that selection programme he selected for body weight at eight weeks of age but Siegel (1963) also measured the correlated responses for several other characters. For example, the genetic correlations between eight-week body weight and thirty-eight-week body weight, sexual maturity and egg weight are given in Table 10 for females and by generation. The heritabilities for the same characters and generations are also shown. The thirty-eight-week body weight and egg weight are consistently positively correlated and sexual maturity consistently negatively correlated with eight-week body weight. Thus it is to be expected that selection for increased eight-week body weight will lead to correlated increases in thirty-eight-week weight and egg weight and to earlier maturity. Selection for low eight-week weight is predicted to be associated with correlated responses in the opposite directions. The changes observed are shown in Table 11. For all three correlated characters the differences between the two selected lines increased and the changes in the individual lines are largely consistent with the sign of the appropriate genetic correlation. Thus the consequence of selection for a single character may lead to concomitant changes in many other characters. Some of the changes may be advantageous in terms of the overall performance of the animal, others may be disadvantageous. The breeder must ensure that overall performance improves and in order to achieve this objective and prevent adverse correlated responses he may have to apply selection to more than one character simultaneously.

Table 10 Heritabilities of thirty-eight-week body weight, sexual maturity and egg weight and the genetic correlations of these unselected characters with eight-week body weight. (Adapted from SIEGEL, 1963, *Poultry Science*, **42**, 896–905.)

Unselected characters	Sex	Heritability (h^2)					Genetic correlation with eight-week body weight			
		P_1	F_1	F_2	F_3	F_4	F_1	F_2	F_3	F_4
Thirty-eight-week weight	♀	0.19	0.48	0.13	0.60	0.49	0.48	1.02*	0.32	0.71
Sexual maturity	♀	0.55	0.53	0.29	0.39	0.13	−0.11	−0.25	−0.23	−0.30
Egg weight	♀	1.06	0.25	0.53	0.49	0.81	0.57	0.32	0.18	0.24

*This value exceeds 1.0 probabaly as a result of error of estimation of components of variance.

Table 11 Change in mean for thiry-eight-week body weight, sexual maturity and egg weight between lines selected for high and low eight-week body weight – females only. (Adapted from SIEGEL, 1963.)

Generation	Line	38 week weight (kg) Mean ± σ	Sexual maturity (days to 1st egg) Mean ± σ	Egg weight (g/egg) Mean ± σ
P_1		3.13±0.37	181.4±16.5	52.4±4.1
F_1	H	3.17±0.39	166.0±19.3	50.2±3.3
	L	2.97±0.38	168.3±18.2	48.7±3.4
	H–L	0.20	−2.3	1.5
F_2	H	3.15±0.38	182.3±23.3	50.4±4.5
	L	2.82±0.35	189.5±19.6	48.1±3.1
	H–L	0.33	−7.2	2.3
F_3	H	3.22±0.40	164.0±23.4	50.9±3.8
	L	2.82±0.36	178.3±22.0	48.7±4.0
	H–L	0.40	−14.3	2.2
F_4	H	3.42±0.38	160.2±17.4	51.6±3.7
	L	2.64±0.23	174.9±31.1	47.4±3.8
	H–L	0.78	−14.7	4.2

5.3 Selection for more than one character

Unfortunately for the animal breeder, it is usually necessary to try to change more than one character at once. For example, the pig breeder needs to increase growth rate and litter size as well as reducing the amount of fat in the carcase and improving the efficiency of conversion of feed into body tissues. In a single population there are three ways of selecting for more than one character. These are:

5.3.1 Tandem selection

This procedure is the simplest and involves selecting for one character for several generations and then changing the objective of selection and selecting for the second character for a further several generations. The method is rarely used in practice because it is many generations before change in all the required characters can be affected, because simultaneous change of the characters is required and because the characters may be genetically correlated and selection for the second character alone may reverse much of the change effected during selection for the first character.

5.3.2 Selection by means of independent culling levels

This procedure involves setting independent thresholds or culling levels for each character to be selected and choosing as parent those individuals whose performance is above or appropriately below as the culling levels. For example, a set of pigs have been measured for growth rate and fat content in the carcase and their values are shown in Fig. 5–1. The pigs to be used as parents are those which combine the highest growth rate with the lowest fat content. The relative selection emphasis placed on each character can easily be adjusted by modifying the culling levels for each character and this flexibility is to some extent determined by the proportion of individuals who must be selected as parents. The proportion will be represented by the number of individuals measured. This method is easily operated in practice and is widely used where computational facilities are minimal and time between measurement and selection short.

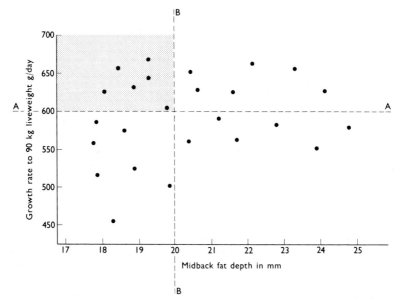

Fig. 5–1 Growth rate and depth of midback fat (measured in the live animal by ultrasonic device) for individual pigs. The culling levels for the two characters are shown as lines A–A and B–B. Those individuals whose values are in the tinted area will be selected as parents.

5.3.3 Selection by means of an index

At its simplest this method involves combining the measurements of two or more characters into a single value for each individual. For instance, the measurements on growth rate and carcase fat content for pigs can easily be converted to values of growth rate of non-fat carcase. This single character can be used as the single criterion of selection. In most cases the calculation of a single value or index is not so simple. To obtain the maximum rate of change for all characters under selection simultaneously it is necessary to combine the phenotypic values for each character of an individual in such a way as to account for the relative economic values, the heritabilities, the phenotypic variances and the genetic correlations of the characters.

As the number of characters included in the index increases the computation becomes relatively complex, and the progress for each separate character declines, particularly in cases where the genetic correlation is opposed to the direction of selection. Selection indexes are used widely but do require access to relatively sophisticated computation facilities.

Theoretically and in practice it has been found that tandem selection is by far the least efficient of the three methods, whilst index selection is about 10% more efficient than the method of independent culling levels.

5.4 Genotype × environment interactions

In planning a selection programme, a breeder has to decide the environmental circumstances under which the programme will be conducted. This is a very important decision which becomes more critical as the range of environments, in which the genetically improved strains are used commercially, increases. Today, for example, semen from selected dairy bulls in the United Kingdom is flown all over the world to sire progeny which will be expected to produce milk under a range of climatic, nutritional, management and disease conditions. The breeder must then decide whether the bulls which have been judged superior on the basis of progeny testing in the United Kingdom are superior in all the other environments in which they produce progeny or whether selection must be undertaken separately in each of the indentifiably different environments. Also he must ascertain whether the heritability of the character selected differs between the different environments. The greatest rate of genetic change will be achieved in the environment with the highest heritability but this will only be helpful if the animals selected in that environment express their superiority when used in other environments; in other words, if there is no genotype × environment interaction.

A genotype × environment interaction may be defined as a change in the relative performance of a character of two or more genotypes measured in two or more environments. Interactions may therefore involve changes in the absolute and relative magnitude of the genetic, environmental and phenotypic variances between environments, so changing heritability. These changes in rank order and in variances are found separately and together and are illustrated in Fig. 5–2. The performance of genotypes between environments can be expressed in the form of a genetic correlation, and for a pair of environments can have a value in the range -1 to $+1$. The correlation, denoted r_g, is a measure of the relative ranking of the genotypes in the two environments after correction for differences in variance between the environments. This correlation can be used, in a similar way to the genetic correlation for two characters in the same genotype and environment to predict the response in one environment as a consequence of selecting in the other environment. Thus measurements of the same character in two different environments should for the purposes of predicting

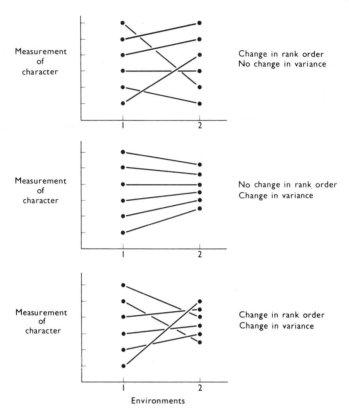

Fig. 5–2 Genotype × environment interactions. The points represent the performance of genotypes (individuals or populations) and the lines join the performance of the same genotype in two environments. (From BOWMAN, J.C., 1972, *Annals of Genetic Selection in Animals*, **4**, 117–23.)

response to selection be considered as two characters. Then the ratio of response for one character in one environment by selection in that environment to the response for the same character in the same environment by selection in a second environment is

$$\frac{R_1}{CR_1} = \frac{1}{r_g} \quad \frac{i_1 h_1}{i_2 h_2}$$

where R_1 = response in environment 1 by selection in environment 1
CR_1 = response in environment 1 by selection in environment 2
i_1 and i_2 = selection intensity in environments 1 and 2 respectively
h_1 and h_2 = square root of the heritability of the character in environments 1 and 2 respectively
r_g = genetic correlation between the character in the two environments.

In general within the usual range of environments found amongst commercial production units, the changes in variance may be sufficiently large and rank order changes sufficiently small to warrant a choice of environments used for selection. In those cases where selection is based on an index of several characters it is usually not necessary to record all characters in all environments and further, though less likely, it may be advantageous to measure the different characters each in a different set of environments. The breeder is often required to carry out a selection programme on the basis of records from commercial units and his choice of environments is then determined not by considerations of programme design and efficiency but solely by the number of producers who can be persuaded to undertake the necessary recording.

There are now many reports of the magnitude of genetic correlation between environments for characters of economic importance in cattle, sheep, pigs and particularly poultry. The correlations do not deviate so far from 1 as was perhaps originally suspected and the environments included have to differ considerably for rank order changes to be important. Extreme differences in environmental rainfall, temperature, photo-period, space, diet and feeding method, and disease exposure are the conditions most likely to result in low genetic correlations.

In determining the number of environments, in which to select in those cases where the genetic correlation is much less than 1, the breeder should first ask three non-genetic questions. What proportion of commercial production is represented by each of the distinguishably different environments and are any of them relatively unimportant? In the economic circumstances likely to prevail in the near future (5–15 years depending on species) are any of the existing environments used for commercial production likely to be abandoned because they are unsuitable for economic or other reasons? Would it be easier (in terms or persuasion, economics or other practical considerations) to persuade some producers to change their environments/systems of production to but one or two standard forms to suit one or two selected genotypes, rather than to select many genotypes to suit the many production environments/ systems?

Answers to these questions, coupled with the magnitude of the genetic parameters, usually enables the breeder to reduce the number of separate strains to meet specific environmental/production systems requirements to very few (2 or 3). However, it does emphasize the advantages to be gained from closer collaboration between breeders and workers in other disciplines (e.g. nutrition, behaviour, environment) in finding the optimum combination of genotype and environment.

6 Inbreeding and Crossbreeding

6.1 Inbreeding

Inbreeding is strictly defined as the mating of individuals who are more closely related by ancestory than the average relationships of all individuals in the population. In many populations mating involving full or half sibs or offspring and parent or even cousins are inbred matings. At one time animal breeders used inbreeding in an effort to concentrate the genes of highly considered individual animals in a herd. A cattle breeder with a bull, which he considered to have particular merit, would use the male for mating two or even three generations of cows in his herd. The bull might be mated both to his daughters and to his granddaughters. By this mating scheme the herd came to contain a high proportion of genes from one animal but the phenotypic results were not always desirable. It was common for some abnormality to appear. This was usually suspected of being caused by some single recessive gene carried by the bull, which became homozygous in the later generations of cows as a consequence of inbreeding. As the bull was a heterozygous carrier of the undesirable recessive gene, it caused no ill effects in him and if the bull had been mated only to unrelated cows the chances of the gene being represented homozygously in the herd were small. Today inbreeding is not widely practised in this way because of its deleterious effects but it is used for other purposes in some more sophisticated and large-scale programmes for poultry and pigs.

6.2 The measurement of inbreeding

Inbreeding leads to the same gene being inherited by an individual from each of its parents as a consequence of common ancestry. This is referred to as the inheritance of genes which are alike by descent, as distinct from alike by state. Thus an individual may be homozygous at a locus because the same gene came from some common ancestor via both parental pedigrees (alike by descent) or by chance because of the frequency of the gene in the population (alike by state). The probability that two genes at any locus in an individual are alike by descent is referred to as the *coefficient of breeding, F.* The coefficient can only be quantified in relative terms, with reference to some particular generation of a population. The generation used as the base point is assumed to have a coefficient of inbreeding of zero. Thereafter the coefficient can be measured in several ways, and two methods will be mentioned here. One method involves consideration of the population size and the other a knowledge of the pedigree relationships of the individuals in the population. The coefficient can be estimated from population size in the following way. For the base generation the coefficient of inbreeding $F_0=0$. For one generation of inbreeding the coefficient of inbreeding $F_1=1/2N$, where N is the size of the population in the idealized state as already defined. For a second generation the accumulated coefficient of inbreeding in the population.

$$F_2 = \frac{1}{2N} + \left(1-\frac{1}{2N}\right)F_1$$

and after t generations the total coefficient of inbreeding in the population

$$F_t = \frac{1}{2N} + \left(1-\frac{1}{2N}\right)F_{t-1}$$

which can be shown to equal

$$F_t = \left[1-\left(1-\frac{1}{2N}\right)^t\right]$$

In practice for various reasons animal breeding populations do not confirm to the idealized state. Therefore it has been suggested and found useful to make use of the *effective population size, Ne,* which is defined as the number of individuals, which if bred in the manner of the idealized population would give rise to the same rate of inbreeding as the population under consideration. Then

$$F_1 = \frac{1}{2N} = \frac{1}{2Ne}$$

Some examples of the formulae for calculating effective population size for population conditions which differ from the idealized state are shown in Table 12.

Table 12   Calculation of effective population size, Ne, for population conditions which differ from the idealized state

---

(*i*)   Different numbers of males and females

$$\frac{1}{Ne} = \frac{1}{4M} + \frac{1}{4F}$$

cont.

(*ii*) Different numbers of male and females and equal family size; the number of
males is less than the number of females

$$\frac{1}{Ne} = \frac{3}{16M} + \frac{1}{16F}$$

(*iii*) Unequal numbers of parents in successive generations

$$\frac{1}{Ne} = \left(\frac{1}{t} \quad \frac{1}{N_1} + \frac{1}{N_2} + \frac{1}{N_3} \cdots \cdots \frac{1}{N_t}\right)$$

M=number of male parents, F=number of female parents, N_1, etc.= number of
parents in generation 1, etc., t=number of generations.

This method of calculating the coefficient leads to an average value for all
offspring produced by the N parents. Individual progeny will have a coefficient
of inbreeding which may vary from the average depending on the relationship
of their respective parents. Calculations of the coefficient from pedigree
relationships gives individual values, which for some purposes, such as
controlling the rate of inbreeding, may be more useful. Suppose for an
individual I, its pedigree is as shown in Fig. 6–1. There are two ancestors, Z and
S, which are common to the parent of the individual I. The direct lines of
descent from Z to I and from S to I have been drawn out in Fig. 6–1. Now the
probability that D and E receive the same gene from Z is ½ and the probability
that they receive different genes is ½. However, if Z is itself inbred such that its
coefficient of inbreeding is F_Z then the probability of D and E receiving at any
one locus the same gene from Z is increased from ½ to $(½ + ½F_Z)$ or
$½(1+F_Z)$. The probability that a particular gene is passed from parent to
offspring is always ½. Therefore the probability that a particular gene in D was
transmitted to A is ½ and from A to I is also ½. Similarly the probability that a

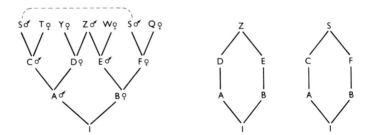

Fig. 6–1 A hypothetical pedigree for individual I, with two common ancestors Z
and S. The pathways of inheritance from Z to I and S to I are shown separately.

particular gene in E was transmitted to B is $\frac{1}{2}$ and from B to I is $\frac{1}{2}$. The total probability that a specific gene in Z was inherited by I by the two pathways Z–D–A–I and Z–E–B–I, so that I is homozygous for the gene is $\frac{1}{2}(1+F_Z)\frac{1}{2}^{2+2}=(\frac{1}{2})^5(1+F_Z)$. Also the total probability that a specific gene in S was inherited by the two pathways S–C–A–I and S–F–B–I is $(\frac{1}{2})^5(1+F_S)$. The total probability that I receives identical genes from its common ancestors is its coefficient of inbreeding, F_I. And

$$F_I = (\tfrac{1}{2})^5(1+F_Z)+(\tfrac{1}{2})^5(1+F_S)$$

This formula can be generalized in the form

$$F_I - \sum_{N_a} (\tfrac{1}{2})^{n_1+n_2+1} (1+F_a)$$

where N_a = the number of common ancestors

n_1 and n_2 refer to the number of generations from the individual to the offspring of the common ancestor

and F_a is the coefficient of inbreeding of the common ancestor

6.3 The level of inbreeding in breeds

The level of inbreeding which obtains in breeds of cattle, sheep and pigs has been investigated, to measure the influence of single animals which were highly considered and widely used by breeders, to measure the influence of importations of a few selected animals into one country from another, and to gain some idea of the structure of breeds. The last objective is important in indicating how improved stock may be disseminated rapidly throughout a breed. For example, WIENER (1961) (*Journal of Agricultural Science, Camb.*, **57**, 21–28) investigated the breed structure in fourteen breeds of lowland sheep in Great Britain. He found that a high proportion of the flocks registered with the breed association had fewer than 50 ewes, used only one ram per year and had existed for less than five years. Such small flocks, so recently established, offer little opportunity to make genetic change by selection. Wiener found that all breeds investigated were arranged in a hierarchy in which a very few of the older and larger flocks supplied most of the rams used, thus effectively controlling any genetic changes that occurred in the breed. This general pattern of breed structure had apparently existed over long periods of time and has also been found in breeds of cattle and pigs, and poultry when breeds were important in that species.

6.4 The genetic and phenotypic consequences of inbreeding

In a previous chapter the effects of finite population size on the change of gene frequency between generations were described. The consequence of forming a set of replicate subpopulations from a base population were also described and quantified. Homozygosity in the subpopulation increased although the expected average gene frequency of the total population is the same throughout all generations. This process of the formation of subpopulations now can be seen to be a form of inbreeding. The subpopulations, particularly when their population size is small (say $N=2$ to 8), are called inbred lines. It is important to know what the effects of the changes in gene and genotypic frequencies are on the mean values of the sub and total populations. The expectation is that if there is any dominance at the loci concerned then the mean value of the total population will decline as a function of gene frequency in the base population and of the coefficient of inbreeding reached when the change in mean value is measured. This decrease in mean value is referred to as *inbreeding depression*. In the absence of dominance there is no inbreeding depression and the mean is expected to stay unchanged.

Several experiments have been conducted to observe what happens when animals are deliberately and closely inbred. A typical experiment was that carried out with pigs by BRADFORD, CHAPMAN and GRUMMER (1958). Starting with a purebred population of Chester White pigs, they divided the herd into three lines, designated MA, PM and AK which traced to three boars named Model A, Purdue's Moderator and Alfalfi King respectively and to six sows. From 1942 to 1945 the performance of the herd without inbreeding was recorded. In 1945 inbreeding commenced and continued until 1950 when in addition to inbred litters all possible crosses of the three lines and three other lines started from different base populations were produced. The performance of the base population and of the three inbred lines, MA, PM and AK, are shown in Fig. 6–2 together with the coefficient of inbreeding of the litters. For all characters, but particularly for the number of pigs alive and for pig weight at 5 months of age, performance declined. There was also some difference in performance between the lines. The level of inbreeding in these lines did not exceed 0.40 but in other experiments where the level of inbreeding reached was much higher, performance continued to decline with the result that nearly all the lines ceased to exist because none of the progeny reached breeding age or those which did proved sterile. It is important to realize that the decline in observed performance in progeny as a consequence of inbreeding is a combination of the effects of inbreeding in the progeny *per se* and of the effects of inbreeding in the dam on the pre- and post-natal maternal environment in which the progeny develop. Maternal effects may be considered less important in a species such as the chicken but must never be ignored. At any stage of inbreeding the coefficient of inbreeding of dam and offspring are different. Thus in the first generation of inbreeding the coefficient for dams is zero and for offsprng may be as high as 0.25 for a brother × sister mating. Similarly, as a consequence of crossing two unrelated inbred lines the coefficient for dams will be high and for progeny zero. From the observation of the performance of their inbred lines and crosses with different levels of inbreeding in dam and offspring BRADFORD *et al.* (1958) were able to estimate the effect of inbreeding on the progeny separately for inbreedng of litter and inbreeding of dam. Their estimates were obtained in several ways but their average estimates are given in Table 13. The effect on the progeny of inbreeding in the progeny was greater than the effect on the progeny of inbreeding in the dam. The decline in performance or inbreeding depression was substantial indicating that dominance was an important element at the loci affecting all the characters observed. These results are highly representative of what happens when animals are inbred. There is variation in performance between the lines presumably as a consequence of

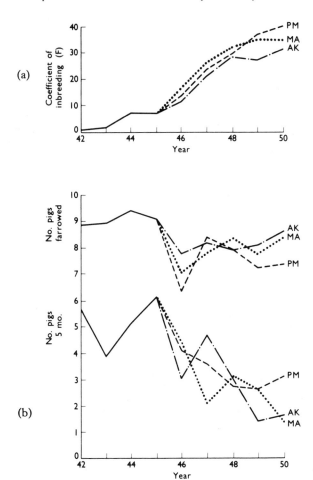

Fig. 6–2 (a) Changes in the coefficient of inbreeding with time for three inbred lines. (b) Time trends in inbreeding of litter and in litter size farrowed and raised to 5 months for 3 inbred lines. (c) (see next page) Time trends in individual pig weights at 56 days and at 5 months and total litter weight at 5 months for three inbred lines. (From BRADFORD *et al.*, 1958, *Journal of Animal Science*, **17**, 426–40.)

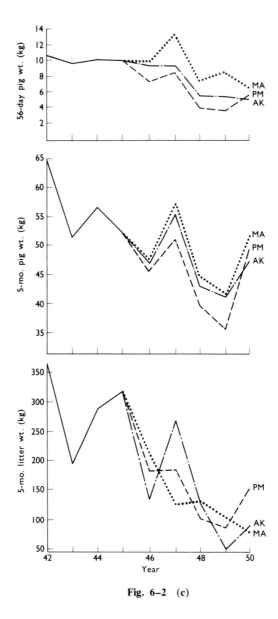

Fig. 6–2 (c)

random drift of gene frequency and nearly all lines decline in performance. The more closely the character affects reproduction and fitness the greater the degree of inbreeding depression. This evidence supports the hypothesis that natural selection favours heterozygotes and that there is a high degree of

Table 13   Change in performance of progeny per 10% increase in inbreeding of litter and of dam. (From BRADFORD *et al.*, 1958.)

| | Number per litter | | Pig weight (kg) | | Litter weight (kg) | |
| | 56 | 5 | 56 | 5 | 56 | 5 |
Born	days	months	days	months	days	months
Inbreeding of litter	−0.20	−0.45	−0.45	−0.50	−2.72	−6.35	−34.01
Inbreeding of dam	0	−0.10	−0.10	−0.32	−0.68	−2.72	− 9.07

dominance, perhaps even overdominance, for all characters closely connected with fitness.

Attempts have been made, albeit always unsuccessfully, to counteract the effects of inbreeding, particularly inbreeding depression, by simultaneous artificial selection applied during inbreeding. The performance of inbred lines developed at the same rate of inbreeding from the same base population with and without artificial selection has led to the conclusion that the artificial selection is entirely ineffective in these circumstances. Another observation of particular interest is that a very small proportion, perhaps less than 5% of all inbred lines started, survive to reach levels of inbreeding higher that 0.80. Such lines often show relatively little evidence of inbreeding depression and can be maintained indefinitely to reach a coefficient of inbreeding of 0.99 and higher. Theoretically these lines should contain individuals which are almost completely homozygous. There is plenty of evidence from poultry and laboratory species that these lines are not as homozygous as the coefficient of inbreeding leads one to expect. The reason for this discrepancy is not known but again supports the hypothesis that natural selection favours heterozygotes and that in those lines which survive to high levels of inbreeding some genetic mechanism enables them to maintain heterozygosity.

As the effect of inbreeding is generally to cause a decline in performance and as so many inbred lines die out after few generations of close inbreeding it may be surprising that animal breeders continue to adopt these mating schemes. Close inbreeding is no longer used by individual breeders with small herds of cattle or sheep. However, several large commercial breeding organizations and Government agencies are using close inbreeding to develop inbred lines of pigs and poultry with high coefficients of inbreeding. They are particularly interested in the few lines which survive for many generations and which because of the effects of natural selection are assumed to be free of many of the deleterious recessive genes which existed in the base population from which the lines were started. These surviving inbred lines are required for their perfomance in crossbred combinations and not as purebred populations to be used commercially.

6.5 Crossbreeding and heterosis

Crossbreeding is the opposite of inbreeding and involves the mating of individuals from immediately unrelated populations, such as inbred lines, strains or breeds. It is a widely adopted practice and used in attempts to obtain the associated advantages of *heterosis*, more commonly referred to as hybrid vigour. Strictly defined, heterosis is the additional performance, if any, shown by the first generation of crossbred progeny (usually termed the F_1 generation which has no connection to the coefficient of inbreeding) above the mean performance of their two parents P_1 and P_2. Sometimes the F_1 progeny performance exceeds the performance of either parent and such crossbreds can be of considerable commercial importance. On other occasions the F_1 progeny performance is less than the mean parent performance and this has been referred to as *negative heterosis*, although this expression does not have general acceptance. The commercial importance of crossbreeds has stimulated considerable research into attempts to understand the genetic basis of heterosis so that appropriate methods of selecting for increased heterosis could be planned and used, and into methods of predicting crossbred performance from the performance of the purebred parents.

Heterosis can be explained genetically in three ways. Firstly there is the 'favourable dominance theory' which states that the F_1 generation is likely to contain a higher proportion of favourable dominant genes than either parent. Undesirable recessives are largely masked in the F_1 generation. However, if heterosis was ascribable to dominance alone, it should be possible to recombine in a homozygous condition, in generations subsequent to the F_2 ($F_1 \delta \times F_1 \female$), all of the dominant genes in some individuals and all of the recessive in others. The dominant homozygotes should have equal vigour to the crossbreds, and when inbred should not show inbreeding depression. It has not proved possible to produce such individuals. An estimate has been made of the increase in yield of an equilibrium population if all deleterious recessives were replaced by their dominant alleles. It was 5%, which is less than the size of increases reported. Dominance is therefore only a partial explanation of heterosis. A second theory, discussed at length by LERNER (1954) (*Genetic Homeostasis*, Oliver & Boyd, London), states that heterozygosity, *per se*, is the explanation. Lerner considers that evolution has established obligate levels of heterozygosity. He considers that heterozygotes have a greater ability to remain within the normal paths of development and that natural selection tends to favour intermediate rather than extreme phenotypes. For an individual and for a population to remain viable a diversity of genetic material must be present. It is implicit in this idea that there is a considerable amount of epistasis to account for heterosis. A third theory states that heterosis results from interaction between genes at the same locus and to this the term *overdominance* has been applied. Though this is a simple and attractive theory, very few specific examples of single locus overdominance have been found. It seems highly probable that there is no single genetic explanation of heterosis but that various levels of dominance, including overdominance, and many types of non-allelic interaction combined in different proportions in different situations result in heterosis.

6.6 The measurement of heterosis

Suppose there are two parental populations P_1 and P_2, which have been developed from the same base population, and that they have been crossmated to produce an F_1 generation. The parental populations are assumed to have different gene frequencies. For example, for one locus the frequencies of the alleles J and j in P_1 are p and q respectively and in P_2 are p^1 and q^1 respectively. Let the difference between the frequencies of the population be y such that

$$y=p-p^1=q^1-q. \quad \text{Therefore } p^1=(p-y) \text{ and } q^1=(q+y)$$

To measure the amount of heterosis it is necessary to compare the mean performance of the F_1 generation to the mean of the two parents.

From Chapter 3, and assuming the genotypic values to be a, d and $-a$ for JJ, Jj and jj respectively, then the mean performance of P_1 can be calculated as $MP_1=a(p-q)+2dpq$.

Similarly the mean performance of P_2 can be calculated as

$$MP_2=a(p^1-q^1)+2dp^1q^1$$
$$=a(p-y-q-y)+2d(p-y)(q+y)$$

The mean parental performance is

$$MP=\tfrac{1}{2}(MP_1+MP_2)$$
$$=a(p-q-y)+d[2pq+y(p-q)-y^2]$$

The mean performance of the F_1 generation can be calculated from the information given in Table 14.

Table 14   Estimation of the mean value of the F_1 generation.

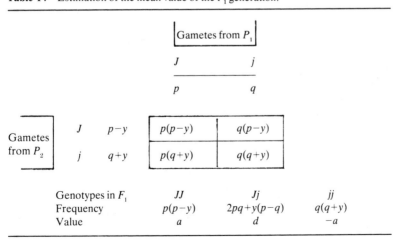

			Gametes from P_1	
			J	j
			p	q
Gametes from P_2	J	$p-y$	$p(p-y)$	$q(p-y)$
	j	$q+y$	$p(q+y)$	$q(q+y)$

	JJ	Jj	jj
Genotypes in F_1	JJ	Jj	jj
Frequency	$p(p-y)$	$2pq+y(p-q)$	$q(q+y)$
Value	a	d	$-a$

Thus the mean performance of the F_1, MF_1

$$=a(p^2-py-q^2-qy)+d[2pq+y(p-q)]$$
$$=a(p-q-y)+d[2pq+y(p-q)]$$

If H represents the heterosis then

$$HF_1 = MF_1 - MP = dy^2$$

The amount of heterosis is dependent on the level of dominance and the difference in gene frequency between the parental populations. The model does not take account of any heterosis resulting from epistasis. If the F_1 population is intermated to produce a further generation, the F_2, then it can be shown that $HF_2 = MF_2 - MP = \frac{1}{2}dy^2 = \frac{1}{2}HF_1$.

The heterosis in the F_2 generation is half that in the F_1.

These relationships can be used to measure heterosis and to predict the performance of populations which cannot be measured directly under certain circumstances. For instance, WIJERATNE (1970) has reported the performance of crossbred and indigenous cattle in Sri Lanka. He recorded the milk yield of the local Sinhala cattle and of their F_1 and F_2 progeny produced by crossmating with bulls of the Jersey and Friesian breeds imported into Sri Lanka. He was unable to record purebred Jersey and Friesian cows in Sri Lanka. However, using the formulae above and the data in Table 15 he was able to predict the performance of Friesian and Jersey cows in Sri Lanka. The heterosis in the F_1 generation can easily be estimated as twice the difference between the F_1 and the F_2 means.

Thus for the Jersey × Sinhala F_1, heterosis=2(1213 −807)=812 kg
and for the Friesian × Sinhala F_1, heterosis=2(1570 −985)=1170 kg

Suppose that MP_1 represents the mean yield of the Sinhala cattle and MP_2 that of the European breed. The mean parental performance, MP, is given

by $MP=MF_1-HF_1$
and $MP_2=2MP-MP_1=2(MF_1-HF_1)-MP_1$

If the appropriate values are substituted from Table 15 the expected performance of the European breeds in Sri Lanka are for the Jersey

$$=2(1313 - 812) - 569 = 233 \text{ kg}$$
and for the Friesian $=2(1570 - 1170) - 569 = 231$ kg

Such predicted yields are very low, but there are reports which indicate that European cattle when maintained in the tropics have very low yields unless special precautions are taken to provide them with environmental conditions

Table 15   The mean milk yield of Sinhala cattle or of their crossbred progeny from matings with Jersey and Friesian cattle. (From WIJERATNE, 1970, *Animal Production*, **12**, 473–83.)

Breed groups	Mean milk yield (kg)
Sinhala	569
Jersey × Sinhala F_1	1213
Jersey × Sinhala F_2	807
Friesian × Sinhala F_1	1570
Friesian × Sinhala F_2	985

which minimize the heat stress, the exposure to disease and the shortage of feed they would normally experience in the tropics. The level of heterosis for milk yield in these crosses is high. By contrast the level of heterosis for milk yield, calf survival and growth rate is usually of the order of 2–10% of mean parental yield for crosses of European breeds recorded in temperate climates.

It can be shown theoretically that the total inbreeding depression observed in lines inbred from one base population is equal to the total heterosis observed when crossbreds are produced by intermating at random between the lines. This is on the basis of the assumption that no lines have been lost as a result of inbreeding up to the time of crossmating. Under these circumstances the average performance of the crosses is expected to equal the performance of the base population.

As with inbreeding, the level of inbreeding in dam and progeny is different for the first, and sometimes later generations of crossbreeding. The F_1 generation individuals may be unrelated (outbred) but be produced by inbred dams. Only when the F_2 generation is produced does a situation arise of crossbred progeny produced by crossbred dams mated to crossbred sires. Since there is heterosis for characters in the progeny, for maternal effects and for sire characters such as libido, and semen production and quality, it is not uncommon to find that the performance of the F_2 generation is no less and sometimes exceeds that of the F_1.

6.7 Crossbreeding in practice

Animal breeders make extensive use of crossbreeding, though this does not usually involve inbreeding first. A large proportion of the poultry, pigs, sheep and beef cattle used for commercial production of meat, eggs and wool are crossbreds produced by crossmating, selected populations, breeds, strains within breeds and less frequently, inbred lines. The terminology in this area of animal breeding can be confusing. Suppose there are four parent breeds, strains or lines A, B, C and D then examples of the various types of crossbreeding are shown in Fig. 6–3.

Fig. 6–3 Theoretical expected utilization of heterosis in progeny performance in various crossbreeding systems (recombination loss is assumed negligible and loss of heterosis assumed complete in *F₂* and later generations of *intense* mating of a cross). (After DICKERSON, G.E., 1973, *Proc. of the Animal Breeding and Genetics Symposium* in honour of Dr Jay L. Lush. American Society of Animal Science, 54–77.)

Incrossbreeding (production of hybrids from inbred lines) was thought to be a likely successful means of taking advantage of hybrid vigour. Several experiments have been undertaken in which inbred lines have been produced from a base population. In the course of inbreeding, some lines are lost and then the surviving lines are crossed in all possible combinations. The mean performance of these crosses usually exceeds the performance of the base population. This is because natural selection, by eliminating some of the lines, has changed the gene frequency of the population of lines so that it is different from that in the base population, and because natural selection has reduced the frequency of the deleterious and less desirable genes affecting fitness. In addition and importantly it has been found that the performance of the best crosses frequently exceeds the performance which can be achieved as a result of artificial selection in the base population. Alternatively the time taken to produce inbred lines, to test the performance of their crosses and to select the best cross (collectively referred to as incrossbreeding) is less than the time taken to achieve the same genetic gain by artificial selection in a single population. However, in economic terms the cost of the genetic gain from incrossbreeding may be higher than for artificial purebred selection because of the substantial loss of inbred lines. For this reason incrossbreeding has been practised in the main only by large commercial breeding organizations or Government agencies, and is now not commercially very important.

Crossbreeding of all types shown in Fig. 6–3 has advantages and disadvantages. Its principal advantage is that the end product may have higher or more suitable performance than any of the parental purebreeds because of hybrid vigour. In theoretical terms the relative performance of different types of crossbreds is shown in Fig. 6–4. In practical terms, summaries of many studies indicate that for several important characters, but particularly reproductive characters, crossbred progeny may exceed the parental mean by between 5 and 10%, sometimes even more. An example in cattle is given in

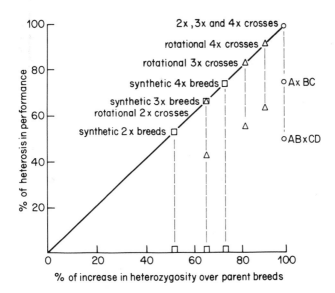

Fig. 6–4 Examples of various types of crossbreeding. Similar terms can be used if the parents are breeds, strains or lines.

Table 16. This sort of advantage accumulated over several characters may mean a considerable total economic advantage for the crossbred over either parent. Often the first cross is not used for commercial purposes but as the female parent for stock multiplication. The multiplier gains the intial benefit, whilst the commercial farmer still benefits from some hybrid vigour in the second cross.

Other advantages from crossbreeding are that it may allow the combination in one animal of several important characters found separately in three or four parent breeds or strains. Whilst this might also be achieved by the development of a new breed, crossbreeding is usually a much quicker method of producing the required animal. Crossbreeding is a very flexible system because the end product can be modified quite quickly by substitution of one or more of the parental breeds by alternative breeds. Also crossbreeding is often adopted because the separate breeds and crosses may be capable of using different environmental niches (land or farm types such as uplands and lowlands).

The major disadvantages of crossbreeding are threefold. First a crossbreeding programme requires discipline and careful attention to the pedigrees of the animals produced. In the absence of these there is

Table 16   Production traits for the Ayrshire (A), Friesian (F), and Jersey (J) breeds of cattle, together with their first crosses and three-way crosses (DONALD, H.P., GIBSON, D, and RUSSELL, W.S., 1977, *Animal Production*, **25**, 193–208).

Parental breeds		First crosses		Three way crosses	
		F_1	Heterosis (%)	$P_1 \times (P_2 \times P_3)$	Heterosis (%)
Live weight (kg) at 18 months for heifers					
A	316	AF 343	−0.1	A×(J×F) 321	−0.1
F	371	AJ 299	4.7	F×(J×A) 330	−1.5
J	254	FJ 328	4.7	J×(F×A) 314	5.2
Milk yield (kg in 305 days) 1st lactation					
A	3329	AF 3980	8.2	A×(J×F) 3832	6.5
F	4023	AJ 3640	7.5	F×(J×A) 3606	−5.9
J	3438	FJ 3869	3.6	J×(F×A) 3665	−1.1
Total milk solids (kg in 305 days) 1st lactation					
A	437	AF 512		8.6A×(J×A) 514	6.6
F	508	AJ 500		7.4J×(J×A) 478	−5.0
J	495	FJ 528		5.2J×(F×A) 502	−0.4

considerable danger that the programme will degenerate into the production of mongrels. Second a suitable use has to be found for the various purebred and crossbred animals which are produced in a crossbreeding programme and which are not the main product of the programme. In planning the programme the production of these individuals must be kept to a minimum and since their performance is likely to be less than that of the required progeny, they will command a lower market value and may even have to be slaughtered at birth unless special uses can be found for them. Third, the farmer, with all forms of crossbreeding, has to purchase replacement stock at regular intervals which leads to all the attendant health and production hazards of stock introduction. The risks can be minimized by having regular multipliers and suppliers who have their stock health status checked regularly, or who belong to minimal disease schemes. Certain forms of crossbreeding such as topcrossing and rotational crossbreeding allow for the replacement females to be 'homebred' and require the introduction of males only (in the case of cattle or pigs this could in the form of semen).

The development of new synthetic breeds is a logical extension of crossbreeding, and if successful can overcome the disadvantages of crossbreeding. However, probably in the long term, most of the hybrid vigour associated with crossbreeding will not be maintained in the synthetic. The choice between synthetic development and repeated crossbreeding then becomes a clear economic comparison of the two systems.

The development of a new synthetic breed is a long term task and patience is essential. The initial enthusiasm among breeders based on high performance resulting from hybrid vigour in the early generations of crossing leads on to a period of disappointment when the new synthetic expands in numbers. This expansion occurs at a time when genetic segregation leads to a considerable increase in phenotypic variation for both type and performance and to some loss of hybrid vigour. At this stage of the development the breeders must have courage, foresight and substantial financial resources to be able to afford to cull all but the most useful animals carrying the required combination of characters. The hybrid breeding companies have adopted similar procedures for the development of new strains.

An important problem for the breeder in developing suitable crossbreds is to try to find ways of predicting the performance of crossbreds from a knowledge of the performance of the potential purebred parents. For only 4 lines there are 12 possible 2-line crosses, 96 3-line crosses and 132 4-line crosses, including reciprocals. Substantial resources are needed to compare the merit of all these crosses, and the number of possible crosses is very much greater for more potential parent lines. To date no very effective method has been found except that in general terms the populations which have the highest performance as purebreds produce the highest performing crosses, and the less closely related the populations the higher performance of the crosses. For those characters for which overdominance is a major cause of heterosis, it is to be expected that crosses of high and low performing purebreds will produce the highest performance.

Having found a high performing cross, the breeder may wish to try to improve its performance. There are three methods available to him. One is to find an alternative combination of lines. For example, if on initial comparison the breeder finds 4-line cross (A ♂ × B ♀) ♂ × (C ♂ × D ♀) ♀ to be the best, he may on further comparison find (E ♂ × B ♀) ♂ × (C ♂ × D ♀) ♀ to be even better. A second possibility is to use one of the selection methods which have been suggested specifically to improve crossbred performance particularly if the heterosis results from overdominance. These methods are called recurrent and reciprocal recurrent selection, but experimental results so far do not suggest that they are particularly successful or efficient. The third possibility is to undertake artificial selection within each of the separate strains in the cross and repeatedly to use the improved purebreds to make the crosses. The first and third methods are widely adopted. As has been emphasized already, it is usually necessary to improve several characters simultaneously. This can be achieved by selection for different characters in different strains and by obtaining some of the combined improvement by crossing the selected strains. Theoretical studies suggest that for those characters with heterosis this is a more efficient method of multi trait improvement than the methods outlined earlier which involve selection within a single population.

7 Selection in Practice

Several aspects of selection have been described in some detail and it is now intended to give a brief outline of one way in which these aspects can be put together as a breeding programme to improve a species for a particular purpose.

7.1 A large-scale poultry breeding programme

Selection programmes do not have to be large-scale operations to be successful but the more populations involved and the larger their size the more chance there is of making significant genetic improvement by selection. An example of the complexity and possible size of a breeding programme for the improvement of poultry for egg laying is illustrated in Fig. 7–1. The programme involves several stages and it is convenient to commence the description by reference to the 'basic strains'. These are separate breeding populations which have been obtained by purchase from other breeders, particularly those who maintain small populations of pure breeds, such as Rhode Island Red, Light Sussex, White Leghorn, etc. These basic strains are maintained in the programme as small populations of perhaps 100 ♂ and 100 ♀ per generation. Samples of these populations are subjected to selection in various ways and for various characters. Thus some strains will be selected by family selection, some will be inbred without selection and others may be improved by recurrent selection to increase heterosis. The third stage of the programme involves testing the various strains in crossbred combinations as 2, 3 or 4 strain crosses. Such testing may involve preliminary comparision of crosses in which up to 200 pullets of each cross are recorded contemporaneously at a single farm. On the basis of initial test results the most promising crosses will be remade and tested in larger numbers on several farms. Such further comparisons may concern 100 ♀ per cross on each of ten farms and a cross would be compared to between 10 and 20 other crosses on each farm. After the results of the final stage of crosstesting the most suitable crossbred is chosen for multiplication for commercial sale. The strains required to produce the chosen crossbred are increased and crossed through three or four generations of multiplication. The comparative performance of various parts of the selection programme can be monitored by means of control strains. The programme might involve between 10 and 20 000 chickens in the basic and selected strains. A further 100 000 chickens might be on test in the two stages of comparing the crosses. The amount of recording and data processing is considerable and it is important to maintain a high standard of accuracy by incorporating regular checks into the recording scheme.

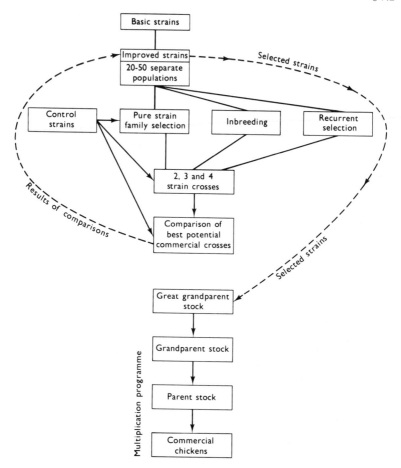

Fig. 7–1 A poultry breeding programme.

7.2 The dissemination of improvement

It is important, once improved individuals, strains, breeds or crosses are identified, for them to be distributed to as many producers as possible, so that they have the maximum effect on the whole population. Little is gained if the selected individuals represent a tiny fraction of the total parent population used. In the farm species until relatively recently a hierarchical structure existed within breeds as was described in Chapter 6. This structure enabled any genetic change in the herds at the top of the pyramid to be passed on, largely by the sale of males to herds at lower strata in the hierarchy. To make use of this structure where it still exists it is important to concentrate selection programmes in the top herds in so far as they can be identified.

As a consequence of the development of artificial insemination, coupled with semen dilution in cattle and sheep and more recently in pigs, it is possible to apply very intense selection to populations of these species and to distribute sperm from a very few of the best individuals. Currently up to 80 000–90 000 doses of semen per bull per year can be obtained and the number of bulls required to inseminate a national herd becomes very small (well under 100 bulls per year to inseminate the cattle of the United Kingdom). On the other hand the responsibility of those who have to select the bulls for use is correspondingly increased, for the effects of picking and using even one bull carrying a recessive defect or inferior performance could be disastrous. Also it is essential to avoid undesirable consequences of inbreeding which might ensue from the use of too few male parents. This is already a problem in some of the smaller breeds of cattle in which one male can provide all the semen necessary to reproduce the population each generation.

Most of the commercial poultry used for either meat or egg production are crossbreds. The rate at which a four strain cross can be produced and multiplied is shown in Fig. 7–2. From relatively few (1331) selected individuals over 30 million progeny can be produced in a period of less than 3 years. Improvement in the end product can be effected either by selection in the strains involved or by substitution of the strains. For example, strain A could easily be replaced by strain E, perhaps resulting in the superior crossbred EBCD.

An important effect of these rates of multiplication is that few selection programmes are needed to improve each species. On the one hand, the cost of the programme can be recouped from a large number of commercial animals derived from the selected parents but on the other hand some replication of programmes may be advantageous for reasons discussed in Chapter 4.

7.3 Some economics of selection programmes

Not only do different selection programmes lead to different rates of response but they require different amounts of resources to implement. Some programmes may require the investment of resources for several years before any response is obtained, whilst others produce an almost immediate response but at a lower rate per unit time when response is averaged over several years. Breeding programmes are now often organized on a national basis and involve the expenditure of considerable sums of money. In order to make the optimum investment, it is important to compare selection programmes in economic terms, such as the cost per unit of response over a twenty-year period.

A standard management appraisal method, namely the discounted cash flow technique, can be used in these cases. The technique involves the assumption of some standard annual rate of compound interest such as 8%. If the first year is taken as a base line, then the discounted value of £1 in each of the following years, for the proposed period of comparison, is calculated. For example, with compound interest of 8%, £1 in year 2 is equivalent to the investment of £1/1.08 =£0.926 in year 1. Similarly £1 in year 3 is equivalent to the investment of

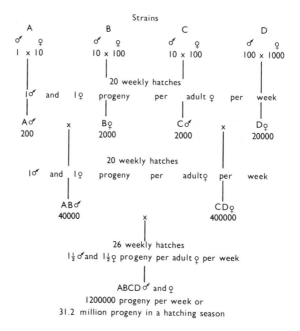

Fig. 7–2 The rate of multiplication for a four strain cross hybrid. From the hatching of the first generation parents to the hatching of the last of the four strain cross progeny would be a period of less than three years.

£1/(1.08)² = £0.857 in year 1, and so on. All costs and returns for each year for a selection programme can be multiplied by the appropriate discount factor and the net benefit of the programme estimated in terms of present-day financial values. Programmes which have different rates of costs and returns can be compared directly on the same financial basis. An example of how this technique works is shown in Table 17. Two alternative selection programmes for improvement of growth rate in cattle are compared. Programme A involves consistent and relatively heavy costs throughout and no improvement reaches commercial cattle for five years. The alternative Programme B requires an initial very heavy cost and thereafter costs are relatively small in following years but improvement does not reach commercial cattle and effect a return for 8 years. The economic assessment of the programmes involves multiplying the costs and returns in each year by the discount factor for that year and summing the net discounted value over years. When this has been done it can be seen that Programme A yields a net profit in year 16 whereas Programme B, which realized genetic improvement for the commerical farmer later, in fact yields a net profit in year 11. Moreover, after year 3 the net advantage is always in favour of Programme B, a result which is unlikely to be predicted from consideration of the relative time taken for the two programmes to realize genetic change alone. This method of making an economic assessment of any breeding programme can be applied easily, assuming any appropriate level of interest. The problem of inflation does not affect the calculation if it is assumed to affect costs and returns equally.

Table 17 Discounted cash flow analysis with 8% discount rate (all revenues are in £'000). (Adapted from HILL, 1971, *Animal Production*, **13**, 37–50.)

Year	Discount factor	Programme A Costs	Programme A Returns	Programme A Net	Programme A Discounted Net	Programme A Discounted Sum	Programme B Costs	Programme B Returns	Programme B Net	Programme B Discounted Net	Programme B Discounted Sum
1	1.000	50	0	−50	−50	−50	235	0	−235	−235	−235
2	0.926	160	0	−160	−148	−198	7	0	−7	−6	−241
3	0.857	160	0	−160	−137	−335	7	0	−7	−6	−247
4	0.794	160	0	−160	−127	−462	7	0	−7	−6	−253
5	0.735	160	0	−160	−118	−580	7	0	−7	−5	−258
6	0.681	160	119	−41	−28	− 608	7	0	−7	−5	−263
7	0.630	160	119	−41	−26	−634	7	0	−7	−4	−267
8	0.584	160	132	−28	−16	−650	7	57	+50	+29	−238
9	0.540	160	160	0	0	−650	7	114	+107	+58	−180
10	0.500	160	181	+21	+11	− 639	7	209	+202	+101	−79
11	0.463	160	273	+113	+52	−587	7	313	+306	+142	+63
12	0.429	160	360	+201	+86	−501	7	396	+389	+167	+230
13	0.397	160	450	+290	+115	−386	7	491	+484	+192	+422
14	0.368	160	572	+412	+151	−235	7	579	+572	+210	+632
15	0.340	160	643	+483	+164	−71	7	673	+666	+227	+859
16	0.315	160	732	+563	+177	+106	7	762	+755	+238	+1097
17	0.292	160	787	+627	+183	+289	7	855	+848	+248	+1345
18	0.270	160	847	+687	+186	+475	7	945	+ 938	+254	+1599
19	0.250	160	913	+753	+188	+663	7	1037	+1030	+258	+1857
20	0.232	160	989	+829	+192	+855	7	1127	+1120	+259	+2116
21	0.214	160	1075	+915	+196	+1050	7	1441	+1434	+308	+2424

Whilst technically it may be entirely feasible to design selection programmes which will lead to genetic change it is unlikely that such programmes will be implemented unless there is a financial or perhaps social benefit in the process. The financial benefit is the net consequence of expenditure on selection programmes set against the additional income derived from keeping improved stock, in a discounted cash flow analysis as shown above. However there are some difficulties associated with determining the potential net benefit of selection programmes. These are

(*i*) some of the costs and benefits are difficult to state in financial terms – for example how does one estimate the benefit of reducing the incidence of tuberculosis in cattle and simultaneously reducing the number of human cases of the disease.

(*ii*) the beneficiary of the selection scheme is not obvious and the benefit may be almost illusory to those most closely associated with the selection scheme's development and implementation. A simple representation of the possible beneficiaries is shown in Fig. 7–3.

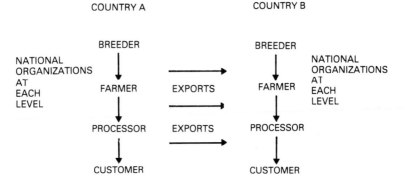

Fig. 7–3 Simple diagram of investors and beneficiaries in selection programmes in two countries.

The breeder in Country A may contemplate selection for a particular trait. The direct benefit to the breeder of healthier stock will be small though there may be a larger benefit to a breeder from being able to sell improved stock to farmers in competition with other breeders with less improved stock. Such benefit is likely to be transient and for a short time. The farmer has some direct benefits from improved stock; essentially more output for the same input. The processor may benefit because he obtains more high quality thus premium products from the stock or its output purchased from the farmer; essentially more output for the same input. The final step in the chain is for the processor to sell to a customer either in the same country or through export in another country. The benefits at this step are either that the processor makes more profit as a result of the improved stock, or that he sells to the customer at a lower price and hopes to sell a greater volume and more competitively with other processors. Country A benefits because it is able to supply a larger share of the world trade and to earn foreign exchange. Gradually the whole system tends to operate in such a way that the benefit derived from the selection programme leads to the customer obtaining the same product at a lower price or a better product at the same price. Eventually competition ensures the customer the better product at the lower price. The result is the benefit obtained from the investment in a free market system. Apart from the difficulty of calculating the benefit, there is also the difficulty of identifying who in the chain has the incentive to invest in selection programmes with a long lag on the benefit and considerable uncertainty about the durability of the benefits. Certainly small scale breeders or farmers are unlikely to be attracted. Large breeding organizations may be attracted though even they may be more keen to concentrate on their direct customers, the farmers. National organizations who can take into account the benefits occurring at all levels of the chain of production and consumption and can afford to wait for the return are the most likely to invest in selection.

Further Reading

DALTON, D.C. (1980). *An Introduction to Practical Animal Breeding*. Granada, London, Toronto, Sydney and New York.

FALCONER, D.S. (1981). *Introduction to Quantitative Genetics*. Longman, London.

HAMMOND, J, ROBINSON, T.J., BOWMAN, J.C. (1983). *Hammond's Farm Animals*, 5th edition. Edward Arnold, London.

HEATH, O.V.S. (1970). *Investigation by Experiment*. Studies in Biology no. 23. Edward Arnold, London.

JOHANSSON, I. and RENDEL, J. (1968). *Genetics and Animal Breeding*. Oliver and Boyd Ltd., Edinburgh and London.

MILLER, R.H. and PEARSON, R.E. (1979). Economic aspects of selection. *Animal Breeding Abstracts*, **47**, 281–90.

SHERIDAN, A.K. (1981). Crossbreeding and heterosis. *Animal Breeding Abstracts*, **49**, 131–44.

Index